POPULAR CRAFTS

GUIDE TO WEAVING

POPULAR CRAFTS

GUIDE TO WEAVING

A L A N & G I L L B R I D G E W A T E R

ARGUS BOOKS

Argus Books Limited
1 Golden Square
London W1R 3AB

ISBN 0-85242-859-6

British Library Cataloguing in Publication Data

Bridgewater, Alan
Popular crafts guide to weaving.
1. Hand weaving
I. Title   II. Bridgewater, Gill
746.1'4   TT848

ISBN 0-85242-859-6
ISBN 0-8019-7723-1 Chilton Ed.

Phototypesetting by En to En, Tunbridge Wells
Printed and bound by R. J. Acford, Chichester

CONTENTS

A woman in traditional Balkan costume, Macedonia about 1887–1900 — the whole costume is hand-woven and embroidered. The base cloth of the skirt is hand-spun cotton, and the apron is a heavy tapestry weave.

INTRODUCTION

Weaving has been described as a fundamental craft, that is to say, a craft that has played a primary role in the history of mankind. Through dress, costume, hangings, prestige banners, rugs and such like, man not only demonstrates his artistic and creative skills, he also, in a visual way, shows his village, his tribe or his town what sort of man he is. Brocaded robes, silken carpets, tribal cloths — weavings of this character all shout, 'Look at me! I'm rich', or 'I'm chief' or suchlike.

And so it is that weaving, especially handweaving, has come to be a uniquely placed cultural craft. Of course, as with all the other traditional rural crafts, weaving survived as a cottage industry up until the eighteenth century, then through a series of 'improving' inventions, it became one of the first casualties of the Industrial Revolution.

By the end of the nineteenth century there were very few individual hand weavers left; small towns and villages had been stripped, and from all accounts, there were not more than six handloom workshops left in the whole of England. However all was not lost, because just as the craft was about to go under, William Morris and his followers stepped in and saved the day.

Soon the Arts and Crafts Revival movement gathered pace and spread all over England, Europe and America.

So how did Morris and his followers manage this miracle? — simple enough, they searched through private textile collections and museums, they encouraged the few surviving hand weavers, they looked to ethnic, folk and tribal weavings, then they used and modified all the designs, techniques and methods.

And so it is with this book, we have drawn our inspiration from the roots of the craft: Czechoslovakian peasant cloths, Norwegian band weavings, Romanian tapestries, weavings from the East, tribal cloths from America and India, cloths from Peru, American Indian blankets and so on.

However all that apart, when we set out the ground work for this book, we were determined that is should be aimed at the insecure beginner in as much as we would have a good solid 'no nonsense' text, and as many step-by-step working drawings and 'hand-on-tool' illustrations as possible. In the Data section we describe the basic weaving techniques, then we go straight in

A detail taken from a Czechoslovakian hand-woven cushion. The motifs are made up from different coloured weft floats, so the weaver would be using several spools of coloured weft yarn. Cloth of this type is sometimes described as 'embroidered', but in fact it is brocaded.

A Navajo Indian woman weaving on a traditional vertical loom — note the use of a shed stick and string heddles.

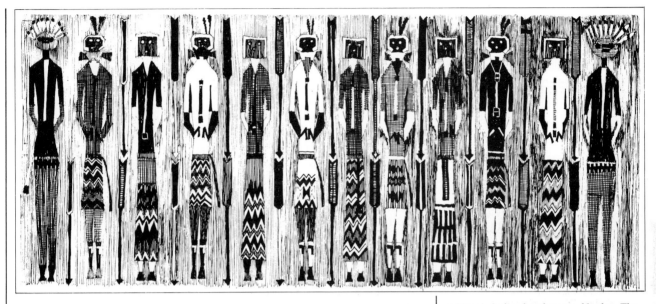

A Navajo Indian hand-woven blanket. The figures and patterns have been taken from sand paintings — the colours are red, black, green and yellow.

with eight very detailed and extensively illustrated, folk and ethnic inspired projects.

By tackling the graded projects in turn, and then using them as launch points for additional weavings, we hope that the beginner will increase his/her weaving expertise and gain confidence. With such projects as, a Scandinavian belt, a Romanian tapestry, a Navajo bag, an American Folk weave rug and an African strip cloth, we feel that not only will the beginner increase his/her craft knowledge, but in the doing will create uniquely personal, prestigious, home beautifying articles.

WEAVERS DATA

TOOLS, TECHNIQUES, MATERIALS, TERMS AND WORKSHOP

When we were first introduced to weaving we both remember feeling somewhat less than self-confident. How would we ever be able to battle through the jungle of jargon words and how would we find our way through the minefield of mystique that surrounds the craft? Of course our first attempts were not so beautiful, just rather lumpy, bumpy, badly woven cloths, but my goodness those first steps were totally absorbing and very exciting.

However, having said that, our first tentative steps would have been so much easier if we hadn't been force-fed with hundreds of obsolete antiquated technique and description words. For example, shaft, heddle, harness and heald — would you believe that they all relate, more or less, to the same bit of the loom? And as for hecks, pirns sley knives and woofs, what can I say? Well now for the good news, certainly it's a help to have all the names for the tools, techniques and bits of loom explained and at your finger tips, but the jargon should not become a burden and get between you and actually weaving.

A warrior's sash woven by the Naga, North India. The weft floats form the pattern, and the cut weft loops, at the selvedge, make up the fringing.

Bearing this in mind, on the one hand we have given you the whole gamut of weaving terms in the Data section, but on the other hand, in the projects, we have reduced all the jargon to a minimum and have tried to call all pieces of equipment and the techniques by their modern international no-nonsense names.

If you are a beginner, our advice is to go swiftly through this Data section picking up on say the 'workshop', 'loom types' and 'yarns' — there is time enough to come back to the Data if and when you have problems with curious catalogue words or outdated suppliers' descriptions.

Apron or Roller Cloth   Taken to mean the cloths on the back and front roller beams onto which the warps are tied. If your loom has cords, these can make for an uneven build-up on the rollers, so it might be better to replace them with strong canvas aprons. Note — all sticks near or in some way fixed to the roller beams are usually termed 'apron sticks'.

Backstrap Loom   A simple, portable ethnic loom found in Central America, the Far East etc. With a loom of this character, there is no frame as such, but rather the warp beam is tied to a tree or post and the cloth beam is tied to the weaver's waist. The backstrap loom has all the usual fixtures: shed sticks, leashes, or a rigid heddle and the like, the only difference is that the weaver controls the warp tension by leaning back on the warp. If you have-a-mind you might make such a loom and weave all manner of items (see projects).

Batten   The swinging pivoted frame, which carries the reed, has a track or race for the shuttle, and is used for beating back and compressing the weft. From loom to loom the batten might be 'overslung' and pivoted on the top rail, or 'underslung' and pivoted below the warp.

Beam   Any round or square section bar or beam that goes across the width of the loom, so there will be a back warp roller beam, a front cloth roller beam, a breast beam over which the cloth runs, structural beams at floor level and so on. Note — the act of winding the warp onto the back roller beam is called 'beaming' or 'beaming on'.

Binder   An American term for the base or ground weft as used in pattern weaving, or a tabby weft thread used to strengthen the structure of a weave.

Bobbin   A tube, spool or quill used for carrying weft yarn.

Bobbin Winder   A hand turned or electric table top device used to wind yarn onto bobbin quills.

Brocade   Sometimes called 'pattern inlay', the pattern or motifs are created by having weft skips or floats (see projects).

Chaining the Warp   Meaning to take the tied and secured warp off the warping frame, and to loop it so that it is contained.

Count   The length per pound of yarn, the size and type of yarn expressed as a ratio between length and weight. For example, a yarn described as a '10's count', has ten 840 yard skeins to the pound weight. However the count system is a weaving black area, with yarns being sold by all manner of curious descriptions. Our advice is to send for yarn samples, then for you to state, in length, just how much yarn you require — 1000 metres, 2000 feet or whatever.

Counterbalance Loom   A loom type where the pulling down of a shaft/harness results in a balanced shaft/harness going up. A loom of this character might have pulleys, see-saw pivoted wooden bars called horses, rollers and such like; the catalogue often describes this type of loom as being 'a loom with an up-and-down balanced shed'.

Countermarch Loom   A loom with vertical or horizontal jacks and a rising and sinking shed. In action, by having upper and lower lams, there is a co-ordinated movement that means you can move warp threads either up or down — each shaft/harness is linked independently to its own, up-and-down, pedals. Note — some weavers favour counterbalance looms and others declare that you can't beat the countermarch action — if you are a beginner, you might get yourself a loom that can be kitted out with either type of harness.

Couper   Meaning the 'Jacks', 'Horses', 'Heddle Horses' etc, that is to say the see-saw levers at the top of the loom — the levers that give motion to the heddle harness.

Crabbing   To crab is to finish off a length of worsted cloth. The fabric to be crabbed is wrapped round a roller and then dangled and rotated in a vat or bath of boiling water — once the fabric has been treated thus for about ten minutes, it is rolled off one roller onto another and then the process is repeated. Finally the fabric is rolled onto an open centred slatted roller and allowed to air dry.

Cross   Meaning the cross-over of threads as worked into the warp at the warp making stage. The 'cross' keeps the warp threads in order and prevents them getting tangled. Throughout the projects we have described the two identical warp-end crosses as being either the back or the front cross, that is to say the cross that goes at the back end of the loom on the warp beam, or the cross that goes on the front roller cloth beam. Sometimes weavers describe these crosses as being 'portee', 'porrey', 'parree' or even, 'parrey' — I've yet to hear two weavers agree as to the meaning of these terms.

Cut   A fixed yarn weight described as the 'Galashields cut', meaning the number of 300 yard units to 24 ounces. Again, there is no need to bother with this type of yarn description, just send away for yarn samples, then tell the supplier that you want such and such a length of a known yarn type — let the supplier do the sums.

A band woven by Guatemalan Indians (Totonicapan). The designs are made up of coloured weft floats — the colours are very bright, purple, mauve, pink, lime green, black and white.

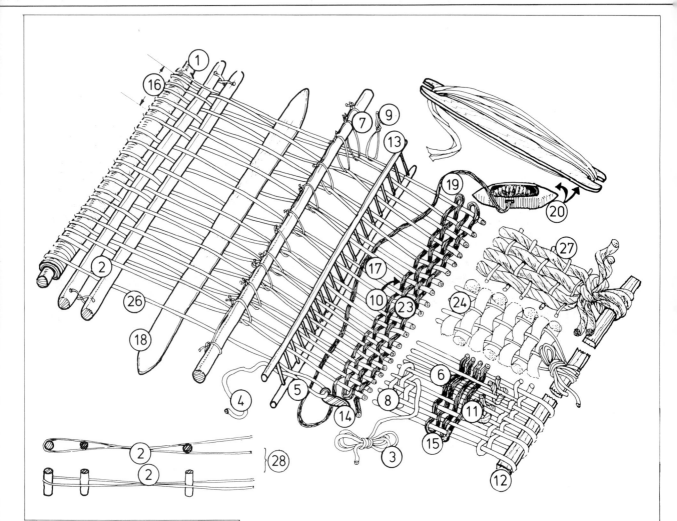

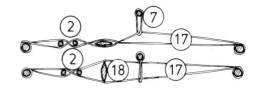

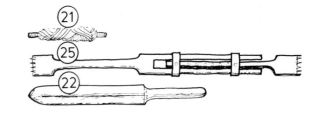

Basic weaver's data, (1) beam, (2) the warp cross, (3) a dolly of weft yarn, (4) a warp end, (5) the act of drawing warp ends through the reed is termed sleying, (6) detail of a brocade weave weft float, (7) leash or loop heddles grouped on a heddle stick, (8) detail showing an inlay, (9) an individual leash heddle, (10) one line of weft is termed a 'pick', (11) individual pile or tufts, (12) a loom stick, (13) the basic reed, (14) a reed hook, (15) selvedge, (16) the number of warp threads per inch width is termed 'the sett', (17) shed, (18) shed stick, (19) one pass of weft through an open shed is termed 'a shot', (20) shuttles, (21) a spool of yarn, (22) a sword or weft beating stick, (23) detail of a tabby weave, (24) a weft faced weave, (25) temple or tenter hook, used to control the warp width, (26) the warp, (27) a warp-faced weave, (28) building the warp or warping.

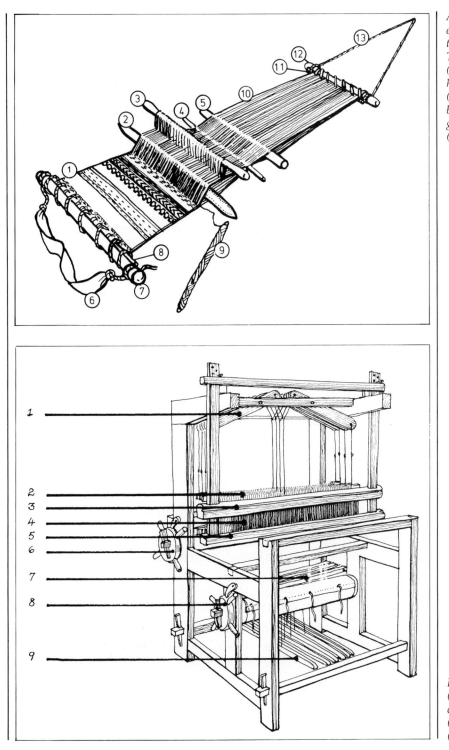

A Central American backstrap loom — note extra supports and beams are needed when the fabric to be woven is wider than 3 inches. The loom parts are, (1) the woven fabric, (2) a batten or sword stick beater, (3) a heddle stick, (4) pattern or pick-up stick, (5) shed stick, (6) the back strap, (7) breast beam, (8) breast rod, (9) spool for the basic ground weft, (10) warp, (11) warp rod, (12) warp beam, (13) suspension rope.

Parts of the loom as used in Project 8. (1) horse or jack, (2) shaft or harness, (3) an overslung batten, (4) reed, (5) shuttle race, (6) warp beam, (7) lam, (8) cloth beam, (9) pedal or treadle

A bobbin winder — this particular type of winder can be clamped to the top of a worksurface.

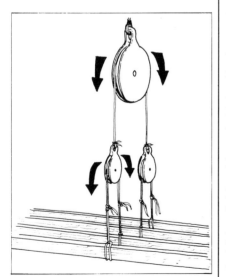

A typical pullies/horses arrangement, as might be found on a modern counterbalance loom — note, if one shaft/harness goes down, this is counterbalanced by another shaft/harness going up.

Denier   The weight standard for counting silk and man-made extruded yarns, so for example a 10 denier yarn will work out at 9000 metres to 10 grammes.

Dent   The slot or space between two reed wires — a reed might be described as having, for example, eight dents to the inch, and a warp might have a dentage, or spacing, of eight warp threads to the inch.

Designing   When you come to designing a weaving, it's always a good idea to take a sketch book to a gallery or museum, search out ethnic, folk and tribal weavings, and use your studies for inspiration. If you are a beginner, don't try in the first instance to weave the largest most complex cloth width possible, but rather spend time getting to know your loom. It's not up to us to say that you should or should not be weaving such and such a type of fabric or hanging, just aim, no matter what you are weaving, to build into your work a quality that can't be achieved by a machine.

Drafting   A diagrammatic and representational analysis of a weave — a drafting plan shows pattern, how the shafts/harnesses are tied to the pedals, the order of pedals, etc. Once again from book to book, and weaver to weaver, drafting methods differ; some show the warp and weft as black and white squares, others show the warp and weft as horizontal and vertical dashes within squares — see our simple drafting plan.

Dressing the Loom   Meaning all the stages that lead up to the actual weaving — putting the warp onto the back roller beam, raddling, threading up, reeding, and tying the warp to the front cloth roller — these are all part and parcel of loom dressing.

End   Or sometimes termed 'end warps', 'warp ends' or just 'warps', meaning a single warp thread,

Figure-of-eight Cross   The two or three-peg cross as made at both ends of the warp — the yarn is wound figure-of-eight fashion round the warping board/mill pegs.

Filling   In American weaving books, the weft is often termed the filling.

Finishing   Any process that the cloth undergoes once it has been cut loose of the loom — see Scouring, Crabbing and Milling.

Floats   Are warp or weft threads that pass over threads of the other set, so a weft thread that passes over say three warp threads might be described as 'a three-warp float'. Note — floats are sometimes termed skips or hops.

Fulling   An obsolete term for milling.

Harness   In America meaning the same as shaft or heddle frame, or in England taken to mean the sum total of all the shafts and heddles.

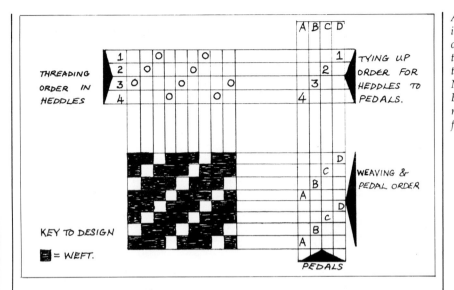

THREADING ORDER IN HEDDLES

TYING UP ORDER FOR HEDDLES TO PEDALS.

WEAVING & PEDAL ORDER

KEY TO DESIGN

☐ = WEFT.

PEDALS

A 'drafting' plan, meaning a diagrammatic interpretation that shows the threading order of the warps through the heddles, the tying up order for the pedals, and the order the pedals are pressed to create the design. Note — the pedals left to right are lettered A, B, C, D and the shafts/harnesses are numbered from the back of the loom to the front, 1, 2, 3 and 4.

Heading   The inch or so of weaving at the start of a length of cloth is sometimes called the heading piece.

Heald   An obsolete term for heddle.

Heddle   The knotted cords, the twisted wires, or the rigid plastic/metal/bone sheet through which the warp ends are threaded — the heddles function as warp supports and selectors and they are contained in the shafts/harness.

The Heddle Eye   Sometimes just termed the 'eye', meaning the hole or loop at the centre of the heddles through which the warps are threaded.

Heddle Stick   Or heddle frame — the sticks or the metal frame that runs through and supports the top and bottom of the heddles.

Horse   Sometimes also termed 'heddle horse', 'couper' or 'jacks', meaning the pivoted or cord — suspended wooden see-saws at the top of the loom to which the harness/shaft strings are tied. On many looms, the up-and-down see-saw action of the horses has been replaced by pulley wheels.

Jacks   Taken to mean the same as 'couper' — in America some looms are termed Jack looms.

Lams   The end pivoted bars underneath the heddles that cord-link the pedals to the harness, or an Old English term that describes the harness/shaft.

Leashes   Loops of cord used in place of rigid heddles, found on frame, ethnic and folk looms.

Milling   A finishing process — the cloth to be finished is soaked in water, worked and matted in a hot water pure soap solution, and finally the cloth is given several clear water rinses.

Pedal or Treadle   Meaning the levers that run under the loom. These levers are cord linked via the lams and jacks to the shafts/harness and they are worked with the feet.

Pick   Taken to mean a single row of weft or filling.

Ply   The number of strands that go to make up a yarn, as in 2 ply or 3 ply, or the word is also used to describe the act of twisting two or more threads together to make a multi-stranded yarn.

Quill   The little paper or plastic tube on which the weft or shuttle yarn is wound — these tubes were once made of quills or reeds.

Race   Sometimes called 'shuttle race', 'batten race', 'beater race', or even just 'shuttle track' they all mean the beading or moulding on the batten over which the warp threads rest, and along which the shuttle runs.

Raddle   A comb-like frame with either wooden pegs or wire teeth. The warp threads are spaced, spread and placed between the raddle teeth so that they are set to the required cloth width. Once the warp threads are in the raddle and well contained with a raddle lid, cap or string, the warp is beamed or wound onto the back warp roller beam.

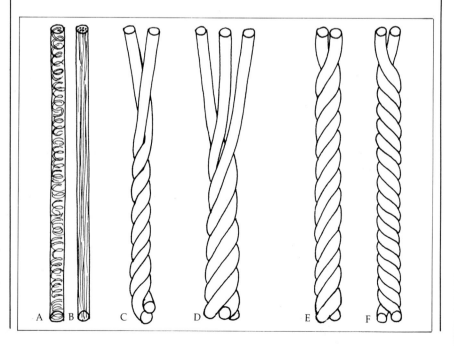

Spin and ply, meaning how a yarn is constructed. (A) a woollen spun yarn, the short fibres spiral to give a soft bouncy yarn. (B) a worsted spun yarn, the long fibres are aligned to give a sleek, smooth strong yarn. (C & D) the ply, the single yarns are twisted to form a thicker yarn. (E) a 'Z' spun yarn has an anticlockwise spin. (F) an 'S' spun yarn has a clockwise spin.

Reed   A steel, warp-spacing, comb. The reed is carried on the batten, and in action it is used to beat back the weft.

Reed Hook   A flat plastic, metal, wood or bone, fish-shaped hook used for drawing the warp threads through the slots/dents of the reed. This whole process is termed 'reeding'.

Rolling On   Sometimes called 'beaming on' — the act of winding the warp onto the back roller beam.

Rolling Sticks/Card   The flat wooden sticks, or the thick card, that is used on the back roller to separate layers of warp.

Scouring   The act of removing grease from wool. The wool to be scoured is soaked in a hot water pure soap solution for at least 12 hours, then it is gently rinsed in clear water. In this instance it is essential that the yarn isn't matted.

Selvedge   The edge of the cloth. The selvedge is strengthened and made firm by doubling up groups of warp edge threads (see projects).

Sett   The number of ends or warp threads to the inch. The 'sett' of a cloth might be described as eight warp ends to the inch.

Shaft   String heddles on two horizontal sticks, or as with a table loom, wire heddles on a metal frame. The Americans term the shaft 'the harness'.

Shot   Taken to mean one pass, or one row of weft through the shed.

Shed   The separation of the warp threads — the 'tunnel' through which the weft thread is passed.

Shuttle   The tool for carrying the weft — there are boat shuttles, double shuttles, shuttles with wheels and rollers, flat rug shuttles with hooks, hook-ended shuttles and so on.

Sley   The Old English term for the reed, or the part of the batten that carries the reed. The act of drawing the warp ends through the reed with the reed hook is sometimes termed 'sleying'.

Spool Rack   Meaning any wooden, plastic, wire or dowel frame that is used for holding spools of warp or weft yarn.

Sticks   Sometimes also called 'warp sticks', 'loom sticks' or 'back and front sticks' — these might be any sticks that are used in the loom, However the term is usually taken to mean the sticks that link the warp to the roller beams.

Sword   A smooth-ended heavy stick used for beating back the weft, or a weft selector pick-up stick.

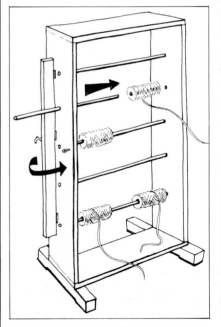

A spool rack, ideally the rack should be sturdy and stable, there should be plenty of room between the pins, and there should be an 'easy release' mechanism so that new spools can be swiftly housed.

Details of a tabby weave. (A) a tabby draft, the weft is shown as black, and the warp is shown as white. (B) the balanced tabby weave. (C) a cross section of the weave.

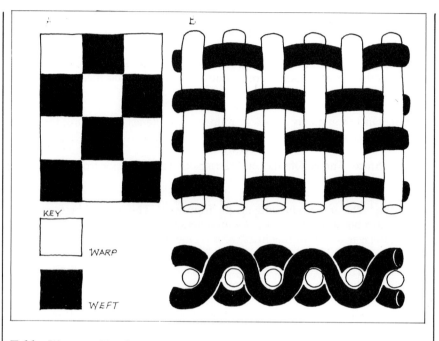

Tabby Weave   Also known as a plain weave — that is to say a weave with an over-and-under-one, balanced warp and weft.

Take-up   The shortening that occurs in a warp's length and width as it is being woven, so, for example, a warp might have a loom width of say 12

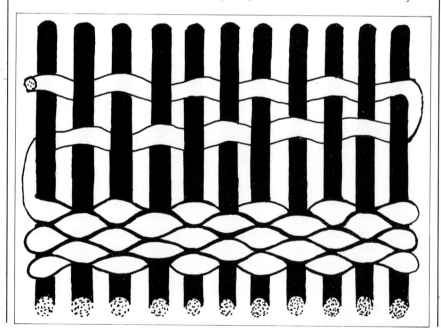

The tapestry weave — note how the dense packed weft completely covers and dominates the loose spaced warp.

inches, but once cut off the loom this same cloth may only be 10–11 inches wide. At the design stage this factor must be allowed for.

Tapestry Weave Meaning a weave that is made up of loose spaced warp threads and a dense packed weft — the warp is completely covered by the weft.

Temple Called also 'tenterhook', 'template', or even 'stretcher', this spike-ended tool is used for stretching out a cloth's width while it is being woven.

Threading Up The act of passing the warp threads through the eyes of the heddles.

Warp The strong threads that run through the loom and the length of the cloth — the threads into which the weft is woven.

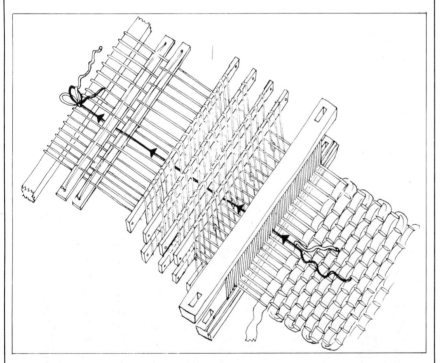

Mending a broken warp thread — see Data text.

Warp Thread Breaks A broken warp thread that occurs during weaving, a broken thread that needs to be patched and bridged. When a break occurs, first find both ends of the broken thread, then take a yard or so of new thread and pass it through the appropriate heddles and reed slot. Now take the end of the new warp that is at the back of the loom, and tie it with a bow to the original broken thread. This done, stroke the new thread towards the front of the loom, match the tension, and then pin it to the woven cloth and continue weaving. When you have woven three or four inches, untie the back bow, draw the original thread through its heddles eyes and reed slot, then pin it to

Mending a broken warp thread — once you have put in a new 'bridge' thread, fix and pin the new thread to the woven cloth.

the woven cloth. Finally, weave another inch or so, remove all pins, and when the cloth is off the loom, darn in all loose ends.

Warping Board   Also warping frames, and a warping mill. These are all adjustable pegged frames on which, or around which, warps are wound and built. The process of making a warp is termed 'warping'.

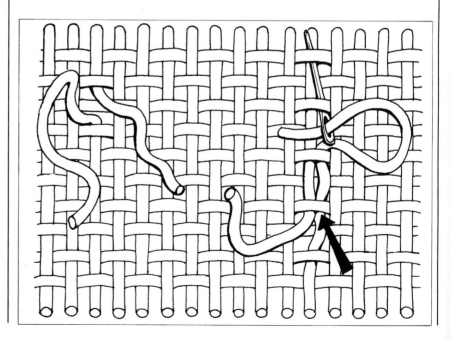

Mending a broken warp thread — when the cloth is off the loom, darn in all broken and mended warp ends.

Weave   Taken to mean the order, scale or sequence of the warp and weft. Sometimes when the cloth is on the loom and in the process of being woven, the term 'weave webb' is used.

Weft   Meaning the threads that are built into the warp, the threads that travel backwards and forwards from selvedge to selvedge. The American's term for the weft is 'filling'.

Workshop or Weaving Studio   We have seen weaving workshops and studios crammed into the most unlikely buildings. For example, our Art school workshop was situated upstairs in a rather dilapidated old house, the lighting was bad, the floors were unstable and storage space varied from dusty cupboards under the stairs to nets slung from ceiling beams. What a mess! but what a workshop, the creative atmosphere was just perfect. And then again, we have seen weaving workshops in school rooms, spare bedrooms, barns, converted warehouses, old churches and front rooms.

As to the ideal working area, that's not so easy to describe because it really depends on the size or your loom/s, your temperament, the weavings that you have in mind, and how much time you want to spend weaving. However, let's say that you are starting out with a small table loom and a medium sized floor loom. Okay, we would say that you could work in a room about 10×15 feet, so a space the size of a double bedroom would be just fine. Now having mentioned bedroom sized areas, we want to qualify this by saying that it's not such a good idea to have a weaving workshop upstairs in a spare bedroom. We say this because looms are heavy, the thump-thump-thump might bring your ceilings down, and in use looms tend to lumber and march about the floors. However, if you feel that your bedroom floor, family and friends are all up to the strain, and you intend to weave in a spare

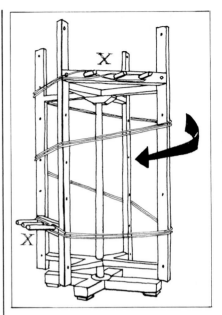

A warping mill — the pegs are adjusted to fit the required warp length, then the warp yarn is wound round the mill and round the 'cross' pegs, as with a warping frame. A mill is only used for making long warps.

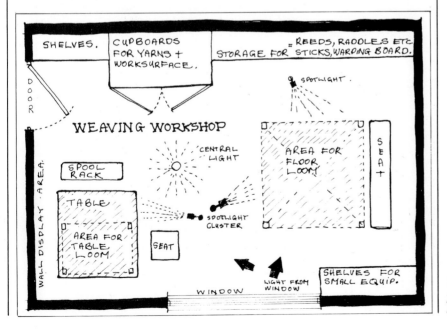

The weaving workshop, or studio. Note the placing of all the storage spaces and work areas, and see how the lighting is organized.

upstairs room, just to be on the safe side, sit your loom on a large sheet of $^3/_4$ inch ply so as to spread the weight and load. And while you are about it, you might cover the walls with some sort of insulation, it helps deaden sound and also makes for a good display area.

Of course your workshop needs a window and electricity, but most important of all, it needs acres of cupboards, shelves and worksurfaces. You need cupboards for yarn, shelves for books, inspirational objects, pieces of small equipment like pens and paints, and you need worksurfaces for designing, drafting, bobbin winding and warp building. As to where in the room your floor loom should stand, the main priorities are space to move around the loom and good lighting. We reckon to have about 2 feet all round clearance, a window to give side or top light, and several adjustable and directional spotlights. So far so good, you can move round the loom without banging into awkardly placed bits of furniture, and when you are weaving you have enough light to see what you are doing.

If when you are threading up or under the loom, the centre of the loom is a mass of cast shadows, you might consider fitting a light to one of the loom's top beams. As for heating, bear in mind that at times weaving can be quite physical, so go for a heating system that can be adjusted to suit the task in hand.

So what else to get into this workshop? You could have a display area — wall brackets for loom sticks and reeds, pegs and hooks for medium-sized bits of equipment, and boxes and baskets for bobbins, quill papers and all the other odds and ends. Finally, bear in mind that although weaving is a dry craft, it is nevertheless messy in the sense that your floor will soon be covered with yarn dust, fibres and scraps of paper, so ideally the floor should be covered with a smooth easy-to-clean vinyl.

'FIRST STEPS' RIBBON CUSHION

LOOM TYPE · BASIC FRAME LOOM WITH A BACKING CLOTH AND PINS

TECHNIQUE · A PLAIN TABBY WEAVE WITH RIBBONS

THOUGHTS ON THE PROJECT

How to start this the first project in the book — it's a bit of a problem. Should we drag you straight in the deep end, and assume that you have a good working knowledge of all the weaving terms, or should we assume that you know nothing, and then bombard you with a whole glossary of weaving words — couper, crabbing, pick, pirn, shot, sley, web, woof and all the rest? We think not! We've both given the shape and contents of the projects a lot of thought — I've watched my wife Gill weaving and working at the loom, she remembers my first feeble efforts when I was introduced to the craft, and, of course, we have both talked to hundreds of beginners and students. Well the message that comes across loud and clear is that often the very thought of weaving is enough to scare away the keenest student or beginner; they have in mind complex, expensive, room filling wooden structures, and acres of pulleys, levers, strings and cordage. but the thing that most puts beginners off is the labyrinth of terms and techniques.

With this in mind, we have structured the projects so that there are as few mystique and jargon words as possible. You can of course concentrate your efforts on making huge complex weavings on a large loom, or you can make simple plain weave items on a frame or table loom — we have shaped the projects so that you can choose. However, if you are a raw beginner, and you don't really know the difference between warp and weft, and you are struggling to come to grips with the very basics of the craft, then this project is for you.

CONSIDERING THE PROJECT

If you have a quick look at all the other projects in this book, and then you compare them with this project — that is the specifications, the working drawings and details etc, you will see that this project is truly a beginner's introduction. The loom is no more than a simple wooden frame, you might use an old picture frame, an adjustable artist's canvas stretcher, or you can knock up a frame in a few moments with four lengths of timber and a handful of screws, no matter. All that is required of this your first loom is that it be firm and made of wood. Our aim with this project is to explain how a weaving can be structured, and also to drop in a few primary weaving terms. Of course you can work this project with card, string, raffia or such like, and just treat it as a learning exercise, the choice is yours. However, we have chosen not only to work the project so that it is a beginner's exercise, we have also shaped it so that the end product is a useful, beautiful item. (See cover photograph and illustrations.)

Okay now for the basics — weaving, in simple terms, is the interlacement of two sets of threads to form a cloth or fabric. The strong threads that run the length of the fabric, or through the body of the loom, are called warps. So individually these threads might be termed 'a warp thread', 'a warp' or even 'a warp end'. The whole bunch, or group of warp threads, is called 'the warp'.

The threads that run across the width of the warp, meaning the threads that travel from side to side, are termed 'wefts', 'weft threads', or 'the weft'.

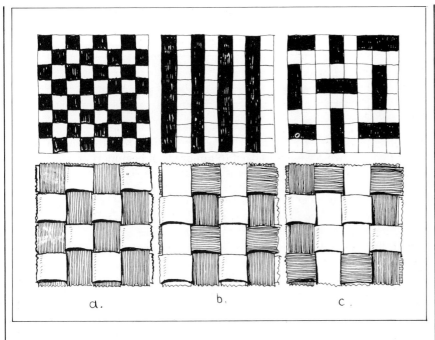

a.   b.   c.

Before you start this project, play around with some black and white ribbons/strips of card, and see if you can come up with several weave ideas. (A) a plain tabby check with black warps and white wefts. (B) a plain tabby weave with alternate black and white warps and wefts. (C) a plain tabby weave with both the warps and the wefts grouped as follows — black, white, white, black, white, white, etc.

As for wooft, woof and one or two other little gems, these are Old English/Norse words that mean weft, don't worry about them.

Now look at the project working drawings and details, and see how the ribbons of the weft go under and over the warp. This the simplest of weaving is known as a plain or tabby weave. See also how the warp ribbons are spaced and placed on the loom, that is to say, note how the ³⁄₈ inch wide ribbons are placed so that there are two to every inch of warp width. In weaving terms, this project might be described as having 2 warps to the inch, or 2 ends to the inch. The arrangement of warp threads to weft threads, the number of ends to the inch, and the relationship between the threads and the loom is termed the 'sett'. With this project, that is weaving a ribbon cushion, there are 2 warp ends to the inch, the weft is the same weight and sett as the warp, the weave is a plain or tabby, and the loom is of the simple frame type.

Now before you go much further, have yet another look at the working drawings, and see how by playing around with the colour of the warp and wefts, it is possible to achieve a sophisticated pattern arrangement. For example, if you say have a weave with black warps, and white wefts, you finish up with a checker board design, or if you have alternate black and white warps, and alternate black and white wefts, you get stripes, and then again, if you group both the warp and weft threads so that they run in the sequence, black, white, white, black, white, white etc, you can achieve a really bold and dramatic block pattern. So by staying with the plain tabby weave, but playing around with the colour arrangement of the warp and weft, it is possible to build exciting, apparently complex, designs.

Now to the project proper, if you look at our gridded working drawing, and at the numbered warp and weft sequences, you will see that not only have we used four ribbon colours, we have also varied the ribbon textures.

The working drawing grid — note the scale of one grid square to one inch. See how, by carefully considering the arrangement of the coloured ribbons, it is possible to achieve quite a subtle design.

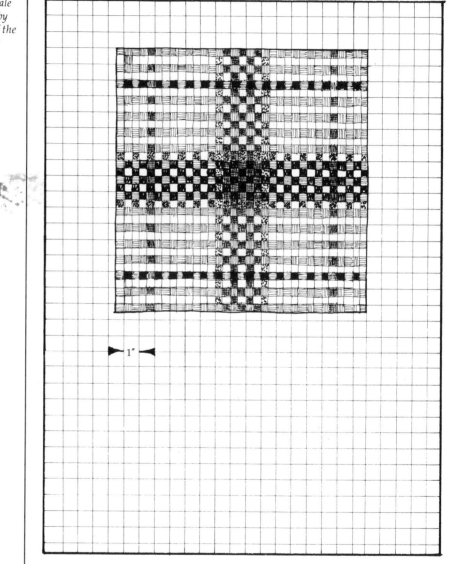

There are four colours, hot pink, apricot, pink and natural, and two textures, grosgrain and velvet.

Finally, when we designed this cushion, we had in mind the heavy drape, luxury of a traditional Victorian type room, so we used muted pastels and velvets. You might use say a hard braid for a Shaker type kitchen chair, or you might cut your own leather strips for a country-rustic feel, the choice is yours.

MATERIALS

For this project, that is weaving and making a 14×14 inch piece of cushion fabric, you will need the following lengths of $\frac{3}{8}$ inch ribbon — 4 feet of pink velvet, 14 feet of hot pink velvet, 40 feet of natural grosgrain, 36 feet of apricot grosgrain, and 4 feet of pink grosgrain. We calculate that with loom wastage, you will need about 65 feet of ribbon in all. You will also need a piece of taffeta or similar backing fabric to cover the frame loom, a square of silk/sateen type fabric to cover the cushion, about 6 feet of the same type of fabric cut on the bias to make up a $1\frac{1}{2}$ inch wide strip, piping cord, and finally you will need cottons to suit.

TOOLS AND EQUIPMENT

For this project you need a wooden frame about 24×24 inches — you might use an old picture frame, a tapestry frame or whatever, as long as it's firm and made of wood it will do the job. And of course you will also need a whole heap of workshop tools like pencils, scissors, colours, workout paper, a tape measure, needles, and a sewing machine.

DESIGNING

First look at our drawings etc, then with colours and workout paper, experiment with various colour and texture layouts. You might also, at this

You need a wooden frame about 24×24 inches, you might use an old picture frame, or an artist's canvas stretcher, no matter as long as it's made out of wood.

stage, visit say textile and costume museums and art and craft galleries, start a sketchbook, start a collection of inspirational magazine clips, and see if you can come up with some fresh ideas. Finally when you feel that you have achieved a good workable design sketch, draw a design plan to size, and indicate colours, amounts, quantities etc.

Place the backing cloth over the frame, and fix it taut with thumb tacks or staples.

THE WEAVING FRAME AND BACKING FABRIC

Start by placing all your inspirational material round your working area, then clear your working surface and set out all your tools and materials so that they are comfortably to hand. Now place the frame on the surface, arrange the backing fabric on the frame, then with thumb tacks, pins or staples, fix the fabric so that it's taut and free from creases and wrinkles. In the context of this project, the frame and fabric structure is the loom.

Now with a pencil and ruler, mark the fabric so that there are centre and border lines, and also indicate the direction of the warp and weft. See how our cushion as illustrated has 29 warp ends and 27 weft picks. You might, if it helps, mark in the position of the various coloured warps and wefts, and also label the sides of the loom, 'back', 'front' and 'side'.

This done, cut all your ribbon into 20 inch lengths, and group them in warp and weft bundles according to colour and texture types. You should have 56 ribbon lengths in all, 2 pink velvet, 7 hot pink velvet, 20 natural

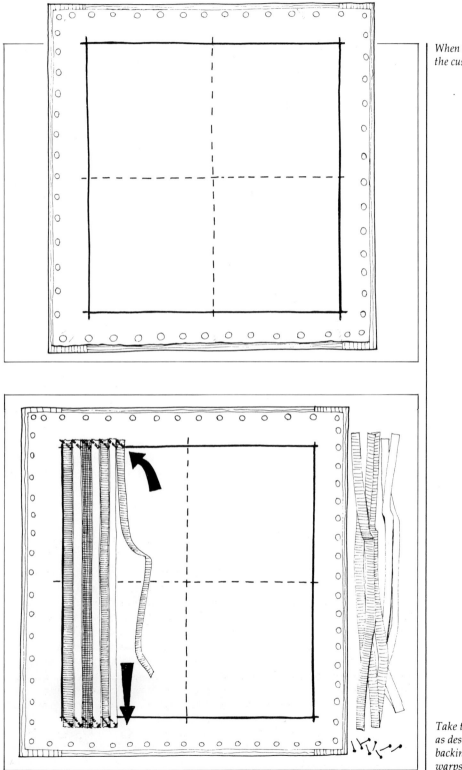

When the backing cloth is in place, mark out the cushion area and find the centre point.

Take the coloured warp ribbons, in the order as described, and pin them in place on the backing cloth — make sure you keep the warps square to the frame.

grosgrain, 18 apricot grosgrain, 7 hot pink grosgrain, and finally 2 pink grosgrain.

PUTTING THE WARP ON THE LOOM

Place the loom fair and square on the worksurface, then place the warp ribbons and the design layout so that they are to hand. Now pin the warp ribbons to the back and front of the loom so that they are parallel to the sides and run in the sequence left to right, apricot, natural, hot pink, natural, apricot, natural, apricot, natural, apricot, natural, apricot, pink, 5 hot pinks, pink, apricot, natural, apricot, natural, apricot, natural, apricot, natural, hot pink, natural and apricot. There are 29 warp ribbons in all (see working drawing). Now in effect the warp is in place, the loom is set, and you can start to weave.

WEAVING

With the frame still square on the worksurface, and starting at the front of the loom and working to the back, enter the weft ribbons across the warp. Place the ribbons, in turn, in and out through the warp, and arrange them with your fingers, as illustrated. The colour sequence of the weft ribbons is hot pink velvet, natural, apricot, natural, apricot, natural, apricot, natural, apricot, pink velvet, 5 hot pink velvets, pink velvet, apricot, natural, apricot, natural, apricot, natural, apricot, natural, hot pink and finally natural. There are 27 weft threads in all. The weaving action line by line is over one, under one, over one etc, as each weft ribbon is woven, carefully comb it into position.

When you are happy with the overall design, take the needle and cotton and tack the ends of both warp and weft ribbons to the backing fabric. This done, free the weaving from the loom, then with a sewing machine sew round the seam line, as illustrated.

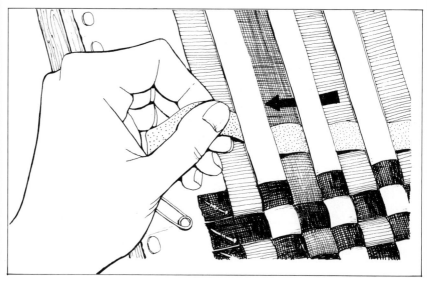

Once the warp ribbons are in place, take the weft ribbons and enter them through the warp in the order as described.

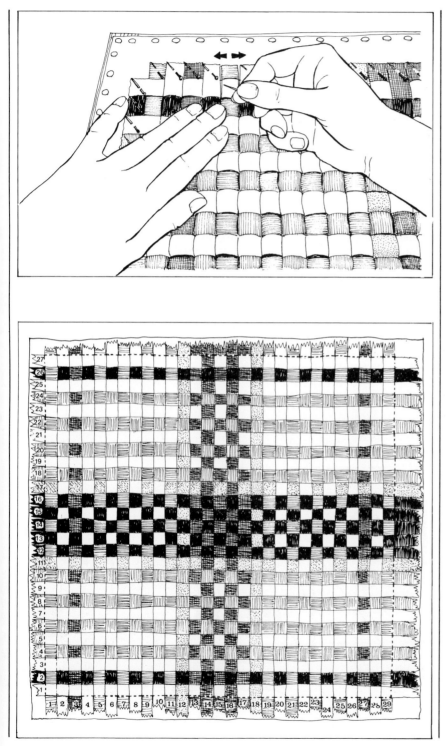

When all the warp and weft ribbons are in place, adjust the pins, and make sure that the overall arrangement is square and nicely taut.

Tack the ribbons to the backing cloth, remove the pins, and check that all is correct.

MAKING THE CUSHION UP

Now take the piping cord and the 1½ inch strips of bias cut fabric, and tack, arrange and machine sew, until you have continuous covered cord that's about 60–70 inches long. This done, place the square of ribbon weaving, face up, on the worksurface, and then place the piping round the weaving so that seam lines match. When the piping is in position, that is with the covered cord facing inwards, tack it in place. Now place the cushion fabric face down on the ribbon weaving so that the piping is nicely sandwiched, then pin and tack. Finally, machine sew the cover on three side edges, put in buttons, studs or a zip, and the job is done.

AFTERTHOUGHTS AND TIPS

This project is primarily aimed at the beginner who has little or no understanding of weaving techniques, so if you feel that you only want to treat it as a learning exercise, you might experiment with strips of black and white card. Label the strips 'warp' and 'weft', stay with the plain tabby weave, but try changing the warp and weft sequences.

At first sight, this project might seem to be too simple; this is not so, by re-arranging the combinations of warps and wefts, it is possible to achieve really complex models for future full-scale weavings.

If with later projects you can't see how patterns work, or how warps and wefts relate to each other, you might come back to a loom of this character and use it as a planning and designing aid.

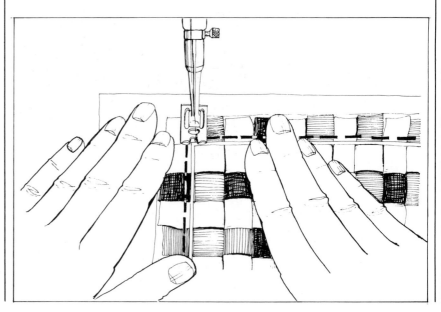

Finally machine sew the ribbons to the backing cloth, and then use the ribbon woven fabric for the cushion front, as described in the project text.

SCANDINAVIAN BELT

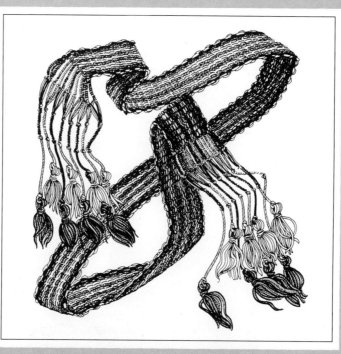

LOOM TYPE · SIMPLE BACK-STRAP WITH CORD LOOP HEDDLES
TECHNIQUE · TABBY WITH WARP STRIPES AND A COVERED WEFT

THOUGHTS ON THE PROJECT

Band, strip or narrow weavings are still being produced in many small isolated ethnic, tribal and folk communities. The Bedouin in North Africa, the Guatemalian Indians in Central America, and the Lapps in Scandinavia, all, to a greater or lesser extent, continue to work and weave narrow strips or bands. As to when, where and why these bands were first woven, who can say? All we know for sure is that there is a positive connection between

Inspirational illustration. A Lapp woman from Kautokeno, wearing a traditional, 'Father Christmas' type costume, and weaving a patterned band with a rigid heddle. Note — the bands that trim the costume indicate the woman's status and clan.

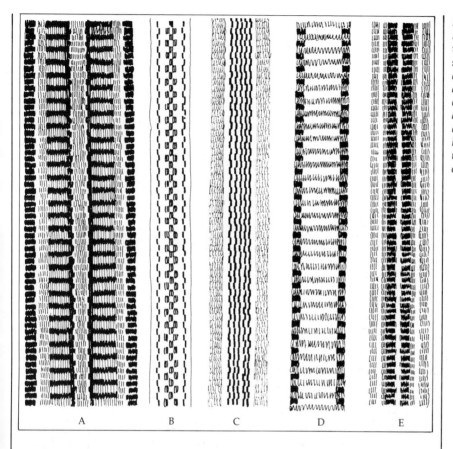

| A | B | C | D | E |

Inspirational illustration. A selection of Swedish warp-faced bands. (A) a wide band with dark brown, light brown and white stripes. (B) a simple white band with a delicate orange design. (C) a pale blue, white and black band. (D) a band with a characteristic 'ladder' design, that is to say, a band with a well defined border and a central section made up of alternate dark and light warps. (E) a common band worked in the classic colours pale blue, dark blue and orange.

bandweaving traditions and techniques, and the nomadic way of life. For example, the Scandinavian Lapps, traditionally, at certain seasons of the year, packed up their possessions and followed the migratory herds of reindeer across what is now Norway, Sweden, Finland and Russia. This mobile way of life, by its very nature, meant that there was a need for a great many ropes, belts, harness-straps and leads, and this is how the band-weaving traditions developed.

No doubt the Lapps now use imported plastic ropes and machine woven webbings, but there was a time, not so long ago, when every single inch of strap and harness had to be worked, spun and woven by hand. With no more than a few sticks and battens, and a supply of handspun yarn, the Lapps made all manner of woven bands. Decorative trim for the collars and cuffs of their 'Father Christmas' type costumes, and belts, braids and head-bands were all woven on simple hook-and-waist, loop or rigid heddle, back-strap looms.

CONSIDERING THE PROJECT

Scandinavian belts and bands of this type, weave and structure were woven in many different ways — with rigid heddles, on small, pack-away looms,

Working with a backstrap loom — one end of the warp is fixed to a hook in the wall, and the other end is tied to the weaver's waist. See how all the individual loop heddles have been gathered and tied to a small heddle stick, this makes for easy warp selection.

with very complex weaves, and so we could go on. However, all that apart, we have chosen to use cord loop heddles, and to concentrate our efforts on a warp-faced weave. The actural weaving technique is described as a warp-faced tabby, and it results in a band that has warp-faced stripes.

Before you start this project, take a trip to the nearest folk/costume museum, and ask to see examples of North European band weavings; it might also be a good idea to search through magazines and see if you can come up with some inspirational designs and motifs. This done, have a long look at our working drawings and details, and see just how the belt has been achieved, that is to say how the emphasis is on a warp-faced design, how the primary 'fat' warps threads are arranged singly and in groups, and how the warp completely covers and dominates the weft. Study the 'loom', and see how in this instance it is no more than a hook/peg on the wall, and a strap to go round the waist.

In this project we show you how to weave a sash type belt, one that is knotted and tasselled at both ends. Of course there's no reason at all why you shouldn't modify the design and add buckles or make the band shorter and call it a tie; this project can very easily be adjusted to suit your needs.

MATERIALS

For this project you need a quantity of white medium, 4/24's cotton yarn for the weft, coloured 3/5's (or thicker), worsted wool for the warp, say 40 feet of white, 40 feet of black, 60 feet of dark red, 120 feet of light red, 40 feet of yellow, and 20 feet of orange, and lastly you need a ball of smooth cotton cord for the various ties and heddles.

TOOLS AND EQUIPMENT

As for tools, you need a 12 inch long flat batten with a hole at each end for the shed stick, a flat wooden batten or ruler for beating back the weft, a dolly, bobbin or shuttle for the weft, a strap or belt to go round your waist, the use of a wall hook, or a massive immovable piece of furniture, the use of a warping frame (see Data section), and lastly you need all the usual tools like a measure, workout paper, scissors and basic kitchen equipment.

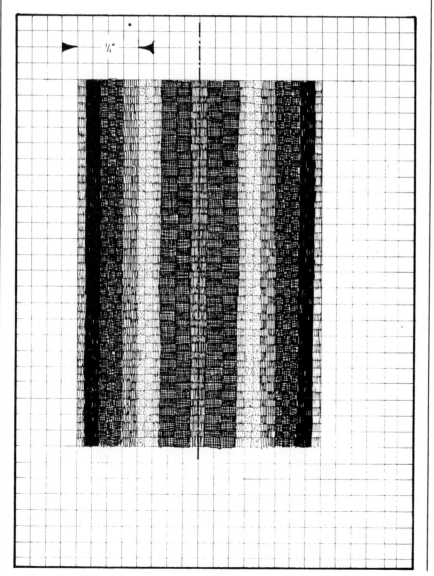

The working drawing grid. Note the scale of four grid squares to one ¹/₄ inch. The colour sequence left to right is, white, black, red, orange, yellow, white, red, orange, red, white, yellow, orange, red, black and white.

MAKING THE WARP

First have a look at our working drawings, and see how the coloured threads are grouped across the width of the warp. Now measure round your waist and allow for cutting, tassels and loom wastage; we reckon that you need a total warp length of about 9–10 feet. This done, set up the warping frame, and using a 9 foot length of string as a guide, arrange the frame pegs, as illustrated in the Data section. The frame ideally needs to have a two-peg 'cross' guide at one end, and a single peg at the other.

Making the warp, tie in the single guide cord.

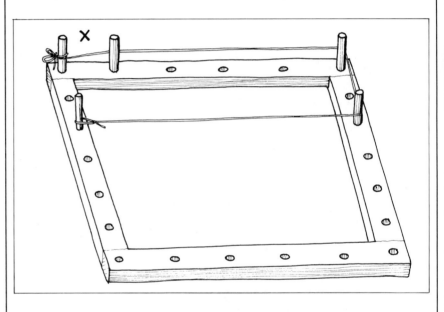

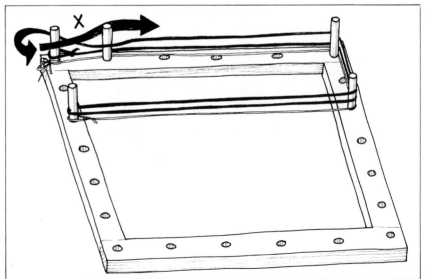

Making the warp, wind your warp yarn through the frame until you have the required number of warp threads — note the 'cross'.

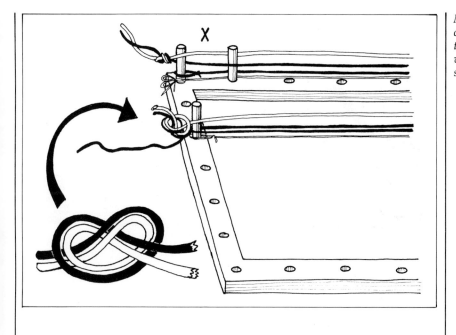

Making the warp — when you want to change the warp yarn colour, make sure that the knot occurs at one end or other of the warping frame, and check that the knot is secure and well clear of the 'cross'.

Now for the most difficult part of the project, take a pencil and paper, and note our colour sequence across the band of white, black, red, orange, yellow, white, red, orange, red, white, yellow, orange, red, black and white, and also very carefully count the number of warps to each colour band. This done, start building the warp by tying a single white thread to one end of the warping frame. Now take this single thread through the frame to the peg at the other end. This done, knot-in some black yarn, and work it, figure-of-eight fashion, back through the frame.

And so you continue, working backwards and forwards through the warping frame until you have knotted-in the required number of coloured warps, and have achieved a well established 'cross' (see Data section). Note — depending on the number of threads in such and such a colour sequence, so the knotting-in will occur at one end, or other, of the frame, no matter, just make sure that every time you tie-in a new warp thread, that the knot is well placed at the turning point of the figure-of-eight.

The next steps need a bit of thinking about, so work slowly, cut yourself a dozen or so 12 inch lengths of smooth cotton cord, and place them so that they are close to hand. Now, bearing in mind how important it is to keep the cross, take four lengths of cord, and loop-off the figure-of-eight warp skein, as illustrated.

This done, take the shed stick, that is the one with the end holes, and push it through the warp as shown. Now, just to make sure that the stick stays put, knot a length of cord over the warp and tie it to the end holes. When you are sure that the warp is well established and secure, slip it off the frame and stretch and fix it across your workshop. Now twist the shed stick so that the figure-of-eight warp turns over on its side and you are able to look squarely down on its width.

Tie the 'cross' with cord loops, then push the warp stick through the cross and secure it with a length of string.

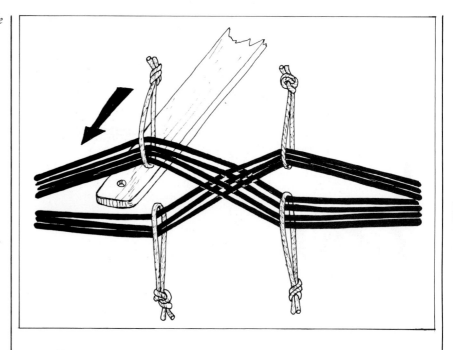

Finally, evenly space the threads, then work across the warp width, and tie-in cord loops to all threads that go under the shed stick.

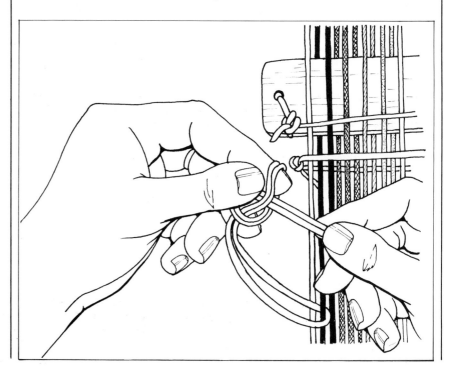

Now tie in cord loops to all warp threads that go under the shed stick.

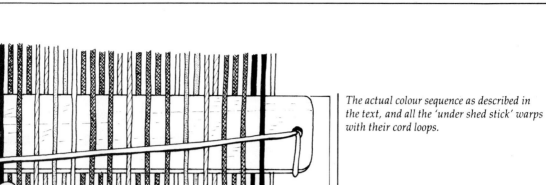

The actual colour sequence as described in the text, and all the 'under shed stick' warps with their cord loops.

One end of the warp is tied to a hook in the wall, and the other end is tied to the weaver's belt.

Now for the big test — put the warp under tension, that is you tie one end to your belt and the other to a hook in the wall as illustrated. Grasp the whole bunch of warp loops, that is to say the heddles, and gently lift them

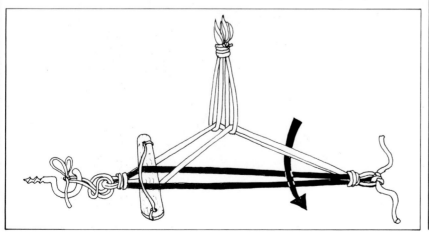

There are two possible sheds, the first is achieved by pulling the heddle loops up, the arrow indicates the passage or 'shed' for the weft.

The second shed is achieved by pushing down on the shed stick, the arrow indicates the passage for the weft.

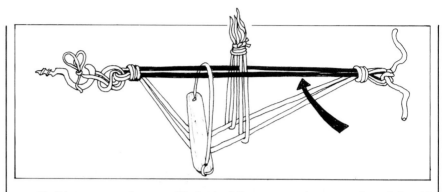

up. If all is correct, when you lift the heddles, every other warp thread should pop up, and when you release the heddles and ease the shed stick down, the same warp threads should drop down. When you are happy that all is correct, and as described, then remove the four cord cross-ties.

STARTING TO WEAVE

First wind a quantity of white weft yarn onto your dolly, bobbin or shuttle, and then arrange your weaving area so that all the tools and materials are within reach. Now set yourself up in the weaving position, that is with one end of the warp tied to your belt, and the other end tied to a wall hook, a large piece of furniture, a post in the garden or such like.

And so to work; lean back in your chair so that the warp is under tension, then gently pull up on the bunch of cord loop heddles. If you now strum the warp threads with the back of your hand, they should twang alternately up

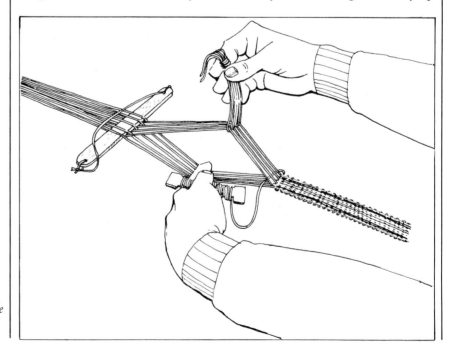

(Note we have not shown all the warps.) The weaving action is, pull up on the loop heddles and throw the weft across.

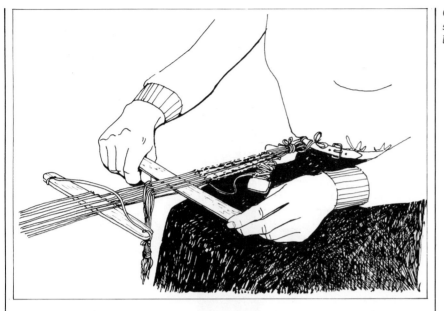

Once the weft has been passed through the shed, check the tension of the warp, and then beat back with the batten.

and down, and the warp should have a clear tunnel or 'shed' that goes across its width. Now take the weft thread, pass it through the shed, and then, at one and the same time, change the shed and beat back the weft with the batten. The weaving action or rhythm is, up with the loop heddles, through the shed with the weft, beat back with the batten, let go of the heddles, down with the shed stick, place the weft in the new shed, beat back with the batten, and so on, until the band length has been woven. Note — it's most important that you keep the band compact, dense and well shaped, so, when you are closing the shed and beating back, pull in on the weft.

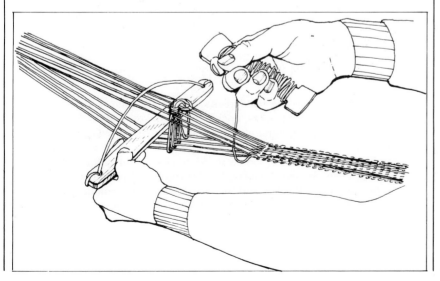

Now make the second shed by pushing down on the shed stick, then pass the weft across.

When the weft is through the shed, make sure the warp width is controlled by the weft tension, then again beat back with the batten/sword.

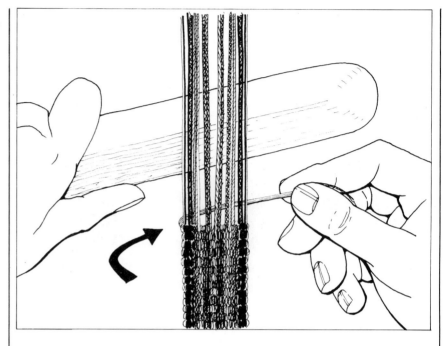

FINISHING

When you have woven the full length of the warp, and the shed is so tight that it isn't possible to enter any more weft, then cut the band free from all its sticks, hooks and loops, and carefully darn in any ends or breaks. Now divide the shaggy warp ends into small groups, then plait or bind each group and knot it off.

Finally, when you feel that you have taken the band as far as it's going, mix a warm water natural soap solution, and give it a gentle but thorough washing. This done, give the band at least three rinses, then weight it at one end, and string it up to dry out.

AFTERTHOUGHTS AND TIPS

You don't have to give the band plaits — it might have a twisted thread fringe, tassels, beads, pom-poms, buckles or whatever, you might even want to give the band a plain square end, in which case the warp ends can be darned back.

If you like this project, but would prefer to change the colour sequence of the warp, or even change the colour and weight of the weft, no matter, as long as the edge warp threads and the weft are the same colour. Note — this arrangement makes for a good finish and ensures that messy weft turns are camouflaged.

If, when the warp is established and set, you bunch and tie the loop heddles to a stick, as illustrated, then you won't have to fumble around looking for individual loops.

If you would rather not use loop heddles, but would prefer to weave this band with a plastic or metal rigid heddle, see the Rag Rug project.

When you are considering just what type of yarn should be used for the warp, bear in mind that a warp needs to be strong, tightly spun, smooth and fluff-free.

Of course there's no technical reason why you shouldn't use subtle pastel colours for the warp, however, our advice is to go for strong vibrant punchy primary colours, and to aim for a traditional contrast of sequence.

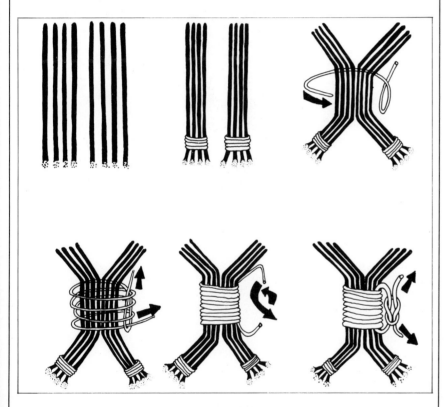

When the warp has been woven and cut off the loom, then the grouped warp ends can be plaited, or bound and lashed.

*A Norwegian Lapp 'travelling' cradle —
traditionally the baby is kept in the cradle
until it is old enough to walk. The
handwoven bands are used to fix the cradle
to the pack reindeer, and the woven motifs
project the child from the 'evil eye'.*

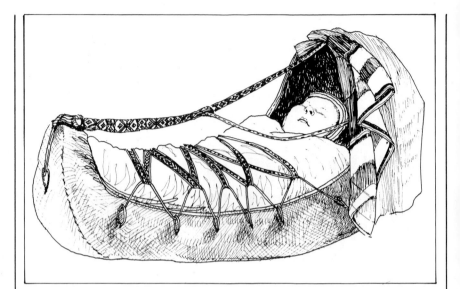

ROMANIAN PICTURE TAPESTRY

LOOM TYPE · BASIC FRAME LOOM WITH A SHED STICK

TECHNIQUE · FREE-FORM TAPESTRY WEAVE IN THE ROMANIAN TRADITION

Inspirational illustration. A Romanian tapestry woven carpet worked in green, mauve, with red, white, yellow and blue details.

THOUGHTS ON THE PROJECT

In very general travelogue terms Romania is a country of extremes — warm summers and long cold winters, rugged mountains and lush forests, busy cities and isolated villages, but most important of all, in the context of this book, Romania is a country very poor in technology and amazingly rich in folk arts and crafts. Picture in your mind's eye very isolated country areas, poor roads and bad communications; areas that for most of the year are literally cut off from the rest of the world. Now add to your picture a peasant population made up of Slavs, Magyars, Turks and Greeks, then fill out the scene with simple wooden cottages, basic self-made furniture, and masses of braids, fringes, embroideries and bold colours. And there you have it, Romania as it was up until the late 1950's.

Inspirational illustration. A nineteenth century Romanian cottage interior complete with loom, weaver and weavings. The woman is working on a traditional loom and making a rug with a weft-faced stripe design. Note that the rugs and tapestries were/are considered to be precious, so they were hung on the walls or draped over the furniture.

Inspirational illustration. An old Romanian carpet from the district of Oltenia. The central area is bright red and all the little birds and flowers are in yellow, blue and brown.

Traditionally the women wore calf length embroidered smocks, fringed braids and belts, and highly patterned embroidered skirts; and there are blouses, jackets, bedspreads, cushions and curtains, all hand woven, brilliantly coloured and wonderfully patterned. But perhaps the most exciting of all are the flat woven tapestry carpets — I say carpets, but in fact they are considered to be so precious that they are usually hung on the walls or draped over tables and beds. For such carpets the Romanian peasant weavers use traditional patterns that are handed down directly from mother to daughter, and so it is that the motifs that are used today are more or less the same as those used a hundred or so years ago.

There are three main areas which give their names to carpets, Moldavia, Banat and Oltenia, and although, broadly speaking, the weaves are similar in structure, the motif styles are quite distinct. For example, Moldavian carpets are rather complex and sophisticated, and show the influence of Russian design motifs, the Banat carpets tend to be rather plain with an overall pattern, but as for the carpets from Oltenia in south-west Romania, these are wildly patterned and brilliantly coloured. A characteristic Oltenian carpet would have a zig-zag edging, borders of stylized leaves, flowers and branches, and finally the whole centre would be covered with naively worked birds, animals and figures, all intertwined with bunches and garlands of roses, berries and blossoms.

Traditionally only the finest wools were used, and not so long ago it was a common sight to see groups of women spinning with drop-whorl spindles. Of course, since the fifties, Romania has been developing its infrastructure and this in turn has resulted in the weavers using machine spun yarns and chemical dyes. However, that apart, the Romanian weavers still continue to make the traditional flat-weave tapestry carpets — poor yarns? harsh colours? maybe, but the designs and motifs remain unchanged.

CONSIDERING THE PROJECT

If you look at the illustration details and the working drawings, you will see that this project has drawn its inspiration from the Romanian Oltenian carpets in that we have taken and used characteristic flower and leaf motifs. Study the working drawings carefully, and see how we have used eight cotton warp ends to the inch (cabled cotton, 9's single, 15 ply), and a 3/5's worsted wool for the weft. See also that although we have stayed with the Romanian tapestry weave techniques, we have chosen to work on a small frame loom rather than a traditional loom. Note — the finished tapestry measures 12×18 inches.

Before you go much further, look long and hard at the various inspirational illustrations, and decide just how you want your weaving to be. For example, you might decide that yes you want to work a tapestry, but at the same time you might want to modify the design and have say a piece of geometrical pattern, a bird or whatever.

Look at the working drawings and details, and see how this particular weaving technique, to a great extent, shapes the design, meaning that the very act of working with several weft yarns and filling in first 'peaks' and then 'valleys' results in motifs that are gently curved and free-flowing. Finally, see our working drawing scale grid of five squares to three inches.

Inspirational illustration. A selection of characteristic tapestry woven Romanian motifs. (A) a sprigs and blossom design from a pre 1900 carpet. (B) a border motif from an early nineteenth century Oltenian tapestry. (C) a characteristic leaves and flower motif. (D) a zig-zag lozenge and ducks motif from a pre 1900 tapestry. (E) a central motif from an old tapestry.

The working drawing grid — note the scale of five grid squares to 3 inches, and see also how the whole design has been related to 'peak' and 'valley' forms.

3"

MATERIALS

For this project you need 300 feet of cabled cotton, 9's single, 15 ply, for the warp (or similar), and you need 250 feet of 3/5's worsted wool, or two ply rug yarn, for the weft. Note — traditionally, Romanian carpets are worked with strong bold colours like red, green, blue and yellow. Avoid sharp acidy colours, rather choose muted primaries to suit your design. As for how much of each colour you need, there are so many variable factors, like how hard you beat back, and how careful, or wasteful, you are when you change colours, that it's almost impossible to give you any firm figures. However as

The loom and weaver — see how the frame loom rests against a wall, and note the various sticks and also the 'hand selecting' weaving action.

a general guide, we reckon on an average weft cover of about 12–18 threads to the inch.

TOOLS AND EQUIPMENT

For this project you are going to need a basic weaving frame, see Data section. Looms of this type come in many shapes and sizes, but commonly they consist of simply an oblong pinewood frame and a handful of battens. The loom that we have in mind has an adjustable horizontal warp tensioning beam, and a top and bottom, nail, peg, slot or spike beam. Go for a loom that is about 24 inches wide and 36 inches high.

You will also need three frame-width battens, a heavy weft beater, a handful of tapestry bobbins, scissors, pencils, loom-sized sheets of drawing and tracing paper, a ruler/measure and a pack of pencil crayon colours.

DESIGNING

Look at our inspirational designs and motifs, and then sit back with your scrap paper and crayons and draw out what you consider to be a good workable design. This done, grid up your loom-sized sheet of paper, maybe even indicating the eight warp threads to the inch, then draw out your design to size.

Now block in the motifs with your chosen colours, and then stand back and be super critical. Are your colours too harsh or too subtle? Is your motif workable in weaving terms? Does the weaving fit the loom? These, and all the other design points, need to be settled at this stage.

THREADING AND SETTING-UP THE LOOM

We must emphasize that although your chosen loom might have warp slots, plastic patent pegs, or even warp beams, rather than the two nail beams, as described, no matter, the overall threading up is as follows. First make sure that the warp beam tension screws are slackened off so that the beam is about two inches from the bottom of the frame, then set out all your tools and materials so that they are comfortably arranged within reach.

Now take your ball of cotton warp yarn, and starting at the bottom left-hand corner knot-in to the first peg/nail/slot. Now, building your warp directly on the loom, thread up-and-down, up-and-down, until you have achieved a vertical web that is spaced at about eight warp ends to the inch.

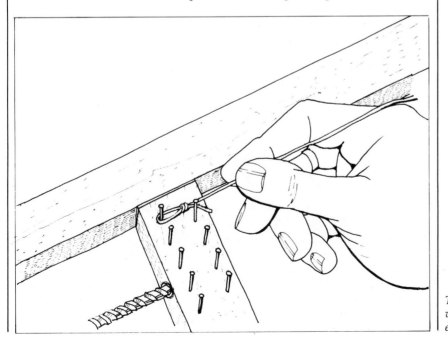

Tie your warp yarn to the first nail, then work a vertical warp webb that is spaced at eight threads to the inch.

And so you continue building the warp directly onto the frame.

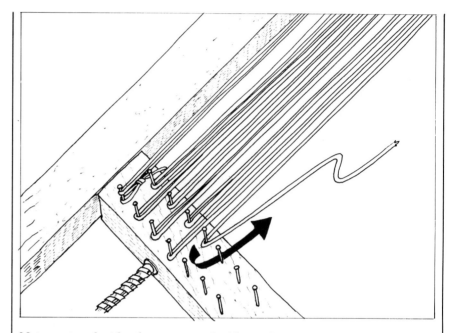

Note — at each side of your warp, double up the two outside threads; this is good weaving practice and it makes for strong firm selvedges. Now tighten up the beam screws and put the warp under tension. This done, enter the shed stick, as illustrated, so that the threads are alternately up or down. Now check that the selvedge threads (two each side) are doubled up, meaning two

Enter the shed stick so that the warp threads are alternately placed up and down.

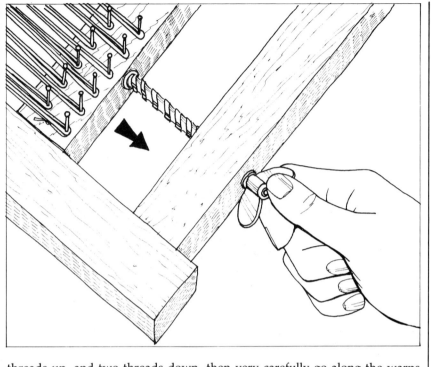

When the loom has been threaded up, tighten the beam screws and put the warp under tension.

threads up, and two threads down, then very carefully go along the warps making sure that each and every thread is well placed and sound.

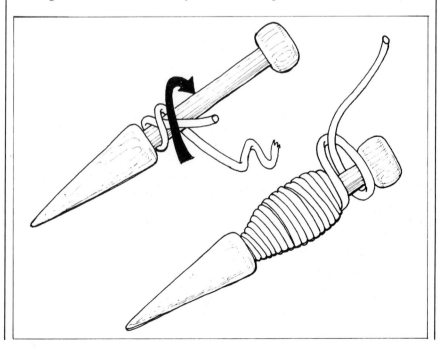

Loading the weft bobbins — note the loop knot that stops the weft unwinding.

Finally, take your full-sized working drawing, or tracing of the working drawing, and place, fix and support it behind the warp with the two pattern sticks, as shown in our working details.

WEAVING

First pin up your inspirational material round your working area, then clear away all unnecessary clutter like bits of left-over warp and scraps of paper. Now check with your colour guide, then load all your bobbins with the various weft colours. This done, start the tapestry, by throwing a few weft strands the full width of the warp.

As you are weaving, check out the behaviour of the warp threads, and try to establish a straight leading edge and firm selvedges. Use the shed stick and your hands when you are selecting warp threads, beat back firmly with the beater, and generally aim to weave an inch or so of full width, well compacted, warp covering ground weft.

THE TAPESTRY MOTIFS AND CHANGING WEFT COLOURS

If you look at the working drawing details, you will see that this particular design can be broken down into what we usually call 'hills' and 'valleys', meaning passages of colour that taper and widen. So the weaving action is — you build up the hills of narrowing colour first, then, when you want to broaden the passage, you leave off that colour, and weave the neighbouring 'valley' areas. It's all pretty straightforward, as long as you work at it slowly and as described. Bear in mind that with Romanian type tapestry weaving, there is no need to have more than a single bobbin of weft on the go at any one time.

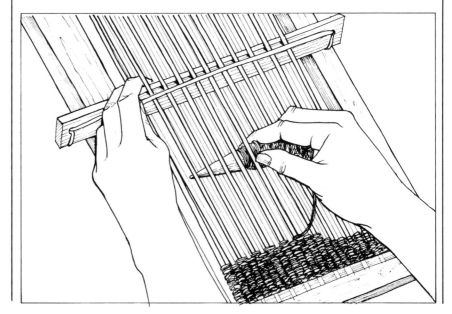

The first shed is achieved by turning the shed-stick on edge — see how every other warp thread stands proud.

Once you have passed the weft through the shed, push the shed stick to the top of the loom, and then beat back the weft with the weighted beater.

As you weave passages of colour and then break off for another colour, make sure that you leave, at the back of the weaving, weft ends that are at least six inches long, then you can darn them in at the finishing stage. Of course weaving in this way results in areas, colours and motifs that differ in texture, so as likely as not, there will be tightly woven areas, bits of loose weave and the like; however in the context of this project, that is weaving an ethnic folk tapestry, these features are desirable.

The second shed is achieved by pushing the shed stick out of the way, and then hand selecting warp threads.

The whole tapestry design must be thought of as 'hills/peaks' and 'valleys' — it is most important that you start the design by building up the 'hills'.

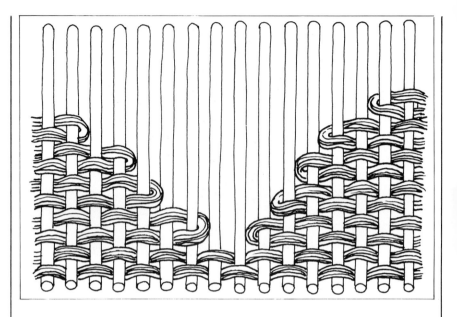

FINISHING OFF

When you have completed the last individual motif, and have just started the ground colour passage, try to re-establish a good firm leading weft edge. This done, weave an inch or so of full width ground colour, then, leaving a generous fringing, cut the tapestry off the loom.

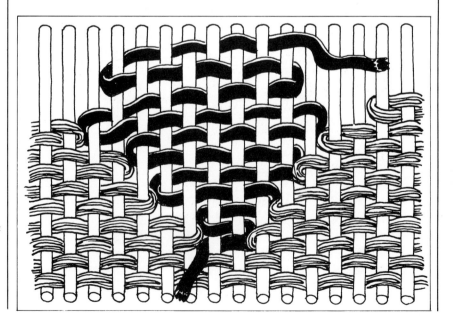

When you have worked the 'hills', then fill in the 'valleys' — see how working in this way gives you a nicely controlled slit-free colour change. (Note — we have shown the weft diagrammatically, in fact it would be beaten hard back, so that the warp threads are covered.)

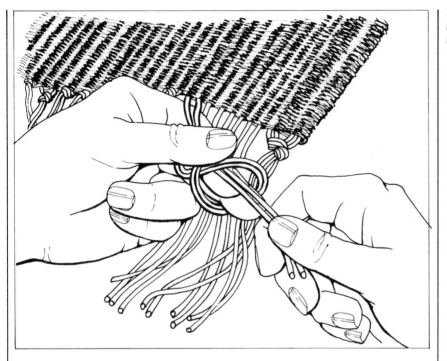

When you have cut the finished tapestry off the loom, knot off pairs of warp threads so that the weft is tightly contained.

Now knot-off pairs of warp ends so that the weft is tightly contained, then take your needle and darn all the loose weft colour-change ends. Finally,

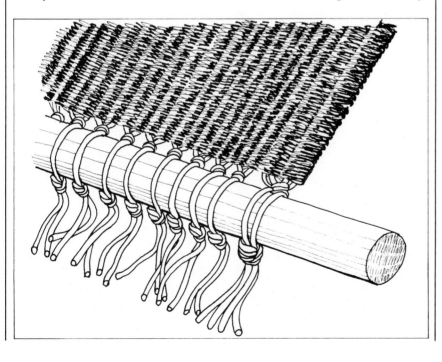

Finally knot-in a 'top' and 'bottom' display stick/rod.

place the tapestry on a clean worksurface and knot-in a couple of display sticks as illustrated.

AFTERTHOUGHTS AND TIPS

Loom types vary a great deal in shape and design so-much-so that your loom might have details and fixings that are quite different from ours — no matter, adjust and modify our project to suit your loom.

If you are a beginner to weaving, our considered advice is to measure up your working area, decide on the sort of weavings that you want to make, say rugs, bands, dress fabric or whatever, then go along to a manufacturer's showroom and have a long look at their literature and demonstration looms.

If you find, as you are weaving, that the weft isn't covering the warp, it is possible that your weft is too bulky — check your materials list.

When you turn the weft at the sides of the warp, that is at the selvedges, don't over tension the weft, just aim for an edge, that is straight, firm and well established.

If your finished tapestry looks to be too buckled or baggy, you can to a certain extent shape it up with a steam iron, or you can even mount it in an all-round display frame.

NAVAJO TAPESTRY WEAVE SHOULDER BAG

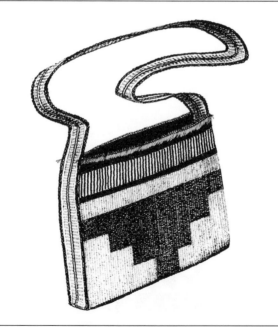

LOOM TYPE · A BASIC FRAME LOOM WITH SHED STICKS AND LOOP HEDDLES

TECHNIQUE · GEOMETRICAL TAPESTRY WEAVE IN THE NAVAJO INDIAN TRADITION

THOUGHTS ON THE PROJECT

The Navajo homeland reserervation of some twenty thousand square miles spreads out across what is now Arizona., New Mexico and Utah. To generalize, the Navajo Indians are shepherds and farmers, and their life-style is one of sheep, goats, desert scrub, and precious little else. What to say about the historical relationship between the Indians and the Europeans, enough I think to know, that it's a shameful story of raids, counter-raids, massacres and reprisals. However the story of Navajo crafts is something again — beautiful silver work and wonderful turquoise jewellery, but of course most impressive of all, are the glorious weavings; rugs, saddle blankets, belts, sashes and ponchos, all woven in a style that has been described as 'strong colour, primitive geometrical tapestry'.

As far as we know, the Navajo knowledge of weaving goes back about four hundred years, when it was learnt from their neighbours the Pueblos, who in turn, it is thought, learnt their weaving techniques from the Spanish. So who knows? Perhaps there are design links between today's Navajo weavings and say Spanish and north African weavings of four and five hundred years ago — it's an intriguing possibility. When the Europeans first came into contact with the Navajo, it was reported that their weavings were made of fine cotton; gradually however, as trade links were established between the Indians and the settlers, it is recorded that the Indian weavers stopped using cotton in favour of wool.

Inspirational illustration. (A) a detail from an 1890's 'revival' Navajo blanket — the contrasting triangles make up a characteristic design. (B) a blanket woven and worn by a Navajo woman about 1875.

Inspirational illustration. An old style Navajo blanket, note that the weave is made of fine wool, the dyes are natural, and see also how the weaver has built up a 'lazy line' of weft, that is to say, the weft has been worked (in some part) with 'hills' and 'valleys'.

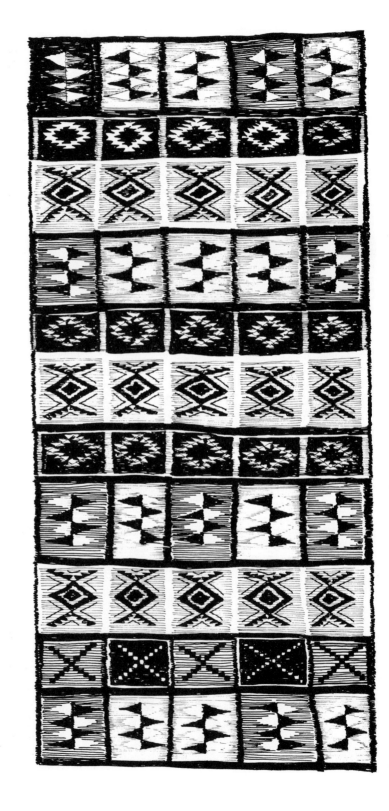

*Inspirational illustration. A Navajo
Germantown rug made about 1890 — the
Indian weavers would have given the trade
yarn extra twist to make it firm and tight.
The colours are red, blue, orange and black.*

As a result of this two-way trade, an interesting state of affairs developed with the Indians unravelling English red Bayeta or baize blankets, and then mixing the yarn with their own homespun. The weavers then wove blankets and rugs that were of such high quality that they were highly valued as trade items. The pity of it is that this trade eventually developed into big business, so much so that by the 1900's the Indians were being encouraged to 'speed weave' and use cheap yarns and chemical dyes. Of course, the inevitable happened, the buyers became disenchanted with the poor quality, loose woven, garish rugs, and by 1914, or thereabouts, the market collapsed and many of the Indian skills were lost.

Now for the good news, since the 1940's, the Indian weavers have gone back to their traditional weaving techniques, and there is now a growing interest in the use of handspun yarns and vegetable dyes. There are now vigorous 'cottage' industries and weaving workshops, with only top grade rugs being produced. A·modern best quality Navajo rug sells at about £2000–£4000, it might have anything from thirty to ninety warp ends to the inch, and it takes about five hundred hours to weave.

Traditionally, a Navajo loom is set up in the open with just a rough stick-and-twig thatch as a shade or cover. The actual loom consists of two uprights banged into the ground, then two horizontal wrap beams are lashed to the uprights so that one is just clear of the ground, and the other is about head height. As for setting up the loom, the warp is either strung directly onto the warp beams, or it is formed on a ground-stick-and-peg warping frame, and then transferred onto two secondary warp-beams. The weft is rolled into balls, not shuttles, bobbins or dollies, and then the warps are hand selected and finally the weft is entered and beaten back with a heavy sword batten.

Characteristically the tapestry woven motifs are hard edged geometrical, that is to say the weft is controlled so that the patterns and designs are squared and stepped, triangles, straight warp and weft lines, zig-zags, diamonds and saw edge pyramids.

CONSIDERING THE PROJECT

If you look at the various working drawings and details, and also look at the inspirational material in the introduction, you will see that we are trying, all the while, to work within the spirit of the Navajo weavers. Okay, so we do use a small frame loom, rather than a lashed warp beam loom, but nevertheless our patterns and techniques are traditional. Look at the introduction illustration of the Indian woman weaving, and then look at the loom as used in this project, and see how in both instances alternated warp threads have loop heddles. See also how bunches of heddle loops can be grasped and selected, and how a shed stick is used.

Now for the most important point that we want to make, if you study in detail the working step-by-step drawings you will see that we fill up the weft line by line, rather than blocking in 'valleys' and 'hills'. This means that when you get to the middle passage, that is the central stepped area of the bag, you will be working with three bobbins of yarn on the same weft line. Note also, how during colour changes, where there are vertical warp lines in the motif, the wefts on the leading edge of the advancing front link-up, meaning that the wefts don't wrap over and share common warp threads;

Inspirational illustration. A relatively modern Indian trade blanket woven with Germantown yarns in about 1900. The border design is non traditional, it was probably influenced by imported European trade cloths.

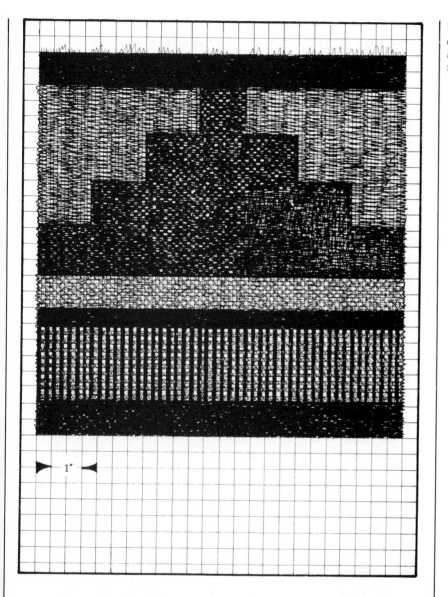

The working drawing grid — note the scale of two grid squares to 1 inch. see also that we have only shown one half of the length to be woven.

but rather they cross over each other between warps. See detail illustrations for right and wrong methods.

Before you go much further, run your eyes over the various illustrations and see how by changing the scale of the woven steps, it is possible to modify our design motifs. Steps, triangles, zig-zags, diamond shaped lozenges, crosses and squares; they are all possible with Navajo Indian tapestry.

Note — we have chosen to weave a small rug that measures about 12 inches wide and 24 inches long, then we double it up and make a shoulder bag. Of course there's no reason at all why you shouldn't make the weaving smaller, larger or whatever — change the project to suit your own needs.

MATERIALS

For this project, that is weaving a strip of tapestry on a frame that measures 24 inches wide and 36 inches long, you will need 300 feet of cabled cotton 9's single 15 ply yarn for the warp, about 250–300 feet of 3/5's worsted wool, or 2 ply rug yarn for the weft.

As for colours, Navajo rugs are usually worked in strong primaries — from bottom to centre, our rug/bag length goes, a band of black, a band of black and white vertical stripes, another band of black, a band of white, a large central stepped motif in bright red, side supporting panels in yellow, a band of black for the fold line, and then finally the other half of the rug is a mirror repeat of the colours as described.

Again, as with the Romanian tapestry project, it is almost impossible to say that you need such-and-such a length of weft yarn, all we can do is to say that you can base your calculations on a weft cover of 12–18 threads to the inch.

TOOLS AND EQUIPMENT

For this project you need a basic weaving frame, see Data section, and our loom detail illustrations. Our homemade loom measures about 24×36 inches, note that the heddle stick is made up from broomhandle dowel, and see how we have used a flat warp stick to establish a leading edge, and how we have used a warp stick for shed control. As for other tools, you need a weft beater, a shuttle stick/s, a tape measure, loom-sized sheets of tracing and drawing paper, and finally, of course, you must have lots of side-tools like scrap paper, pencils and colours.

DESIGNING AND FIRST STEPS

As with all the other projects, start by searching out inspirational and guide material; so for instance, you might take a trip to a suitable museum and see if you can have a close-up look at examples of Navajo Indian rugs and weavings. (Note — The Ethnological Museum in Cambridge, England, has a wonderful collection of early rugs.) When you do get to see some old rugs, study the weaves, and see how the yarns are structured, and how the design motifs are made up of triangles, step-edge diamonds, saw-edges, crooks and the like.

When you feel that you have some understanding and appreciation of what it is that makes for a good Navajo rug, weaves, materials, structure, colour etc, then sit down with a measure, a stack of scrap paper and some colours, and see if you can come up with an inspired design. This done, have a good look and see how our modest length has been turned into a bag.

Finally, see our project specifications and revise, adjust and modify, as you think fit, then draw the design to size on some gridded paper.

The loom and weaver — note the arrangement of the shed and loop heddle sticks.

THREADING AND SETTING-UP THE LOOM

Pin your inspirational material up round your working area, then set out all your tools and materials so that they are close to hand. Now rest the frame loom flat on a clean worksurface and then be ready with the warp yarn, measure and scissors. Note that this warp has doubled up selvedge threads, but otherwise the warps are spaced and sett to eight threads to the inch.

Take the warping yarn and build the warp figure-of-eight fashion, directly onto the frame — see how the thickness of the frame gives the warp a natural shed.

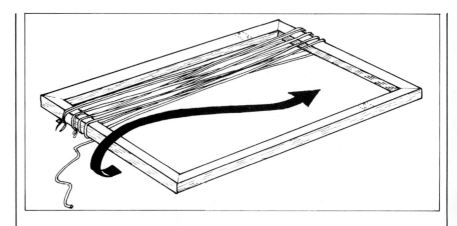

Start by taking the warp yarn, knotting it on to one end of the frame, and then building the warp, figure-of-eight fashion, as illustrated. See how the thickness of the frame-wood gives the warp a natural shed, and how the very process of building the warp in this way ensures that the warps are set alternately up and down. Of course there are any number of little points to watch and keep check on; for example, when you have to link in a new length of warp yarn, you must make sure that the knot occurs at one end or other of the frame.

You might also, at this stage, build into the warp one or more shed sticks — these can be removed during the weaving, if and when the warp tension needs to be eased — see illustration details. And so you continue, until you have built the complete 100 thread warp mesh. This allows for 96 warps, that is eight threads to the inch and doubled up selvedge threads (two doubled up threads each side of the warp).

Now rest the heddle stick on the two little angle brackets/pegs, as illustrated, and start to knot-in the loop heddle selectors. Working from left to right across the width of the loom, and taking the doubled up selvedge warps to be single threads, select and knot-in smooth cotton heddles to every other warp thread. Note — see how the loops are held and contained on the heddle stick.

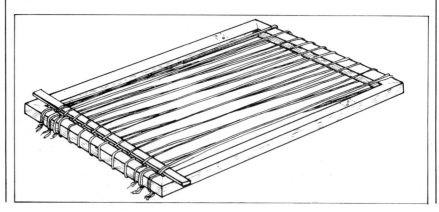

Now push a stick through the warp to give it tension.

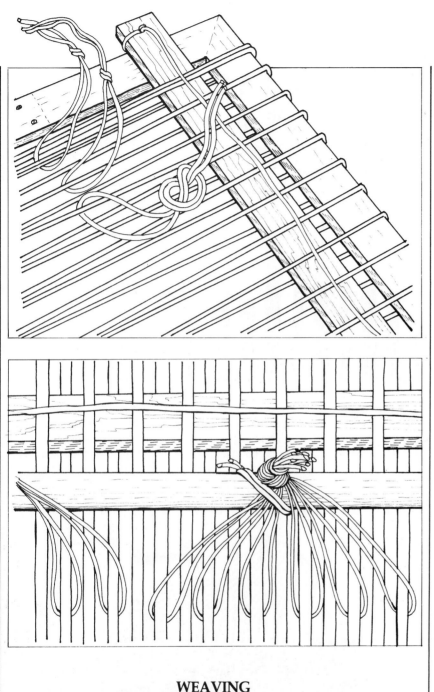

Push the warp stick out of the way to the bottom of the loom, push a shed stick through the warp, then tie heddle loops to all warp threads that go under the shed stick, that is to say alternate threads.

Once the loop heddles are in place, gather them in bundles according to your design, then lash them to a heddle stick.

WEAVING

Start by checking with your design plan and colour guide, then load your shuttle stick with a suitable starter weft. The weaving action for the first shed is, pull on the heddle loops, throw the weft across, close the shed and beat back. For the second shed you turn the shed stick on its side, throw the weft across and then beat back. Once you have got the feel of the loom action and you understand how the two sheds open and close, then start the tapestry by

Just prior to weaving, take a felt tip marker, or a pencil, and mark out the various risers and steps of the design, mark individual warp threads so that they correspond with the design plan. Note — see how the design plan is fixed directly to the back of the weaving frame.

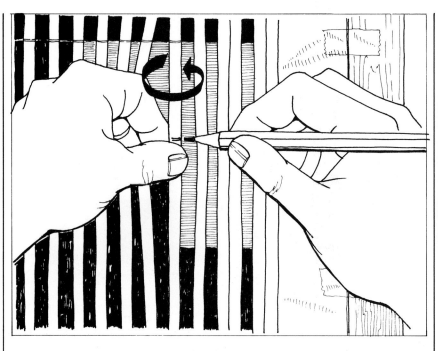

throwing across a dozen passes of weft. Aim to weave an inch of plain, warp-width, tapestry. Of course as you are weaving you will have to keep adjusting the weft so that you neither pull in the sides of the warp and cause waisting, nor let the weft be so slack that it loops up on the surface. The

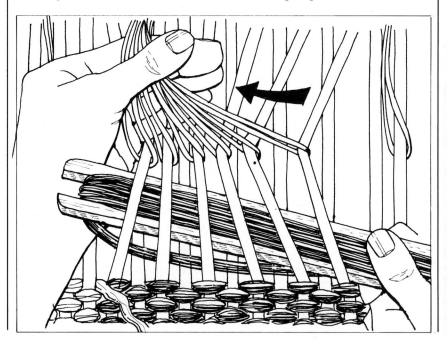

There are two possible sheds, the first is achieved by pulling the heddle loops up and out.

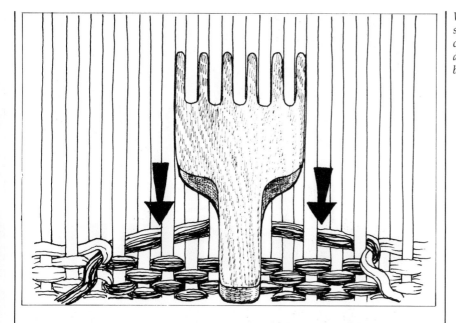

When the weft is in place, close down the shed, and beat back the weft with a weighted claw beater. Note — this illustration is diagrammatical, in fact the weft would be beaten back so as to cover the warp.

weaving process is one of rhythm, and eye, mind and hand co-ordination. If you find that the very action of beating down the weft and changing sheds pulls in the sides of the warp, then instead of placing the weft straight through the shed, rather set it in an arc and then beat back.

When you have achieved an inch, or thereabouts, of well set-up and

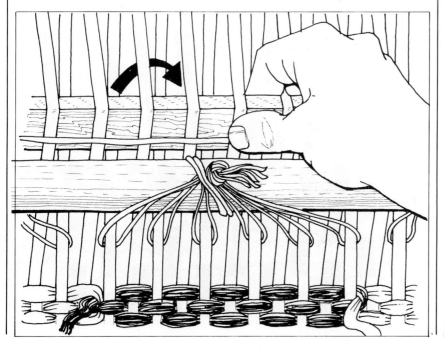

The second of the two sheds is achieved by releasing the loop heddles and turning the shed-stick on edge.

It is most important that when you are building up blocks of say two colours, that you interlock weft passes. Note — the warps are shown as black.

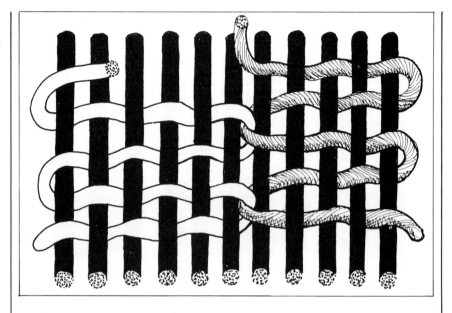

compacted tapestry, then look to your design plan and be ready to weave the band of warp striping.

Load your two chosen weft colours on two shuttle sticks, then throw the two colours alternately the full width of the warp. If you stay with this sequence, and beat back firmly, you will see that it results in an area of nicely defined vertical striping. And so you continue to weave, that is throwing

If, as you are building up neighbouring blocks of colour, you fail to interlock weft passes, there will be vertical slits in the finished weaving — some weavers work in this way and either use the slits as a design feature, or darn the slits when the weaving is off the loom.

across two weft colours until you have achieved about 2½ inches of weft striping. This done, go back to your starter colour and weave a 1½ inch band, and follow this up with a 2 inch band of another colour.

Now for the most exciting passage of the tapestry, that is the central stepped motif. Load your stick shuttles with the chosen weft colour (we used red, see our colour guide), then start the motif by weaving a 1½ inch band. If you now have a look at the working design, as illustrated, you will see that this 1½ inches of red is in fact the first of the four steps that go to make up the motif. Now load two more stick shuttles with another weft colour (yellow, see our colour guide), then be ready to weave the supporting areas.

First measure about 1½ inches in from each side of the tapestry, and mark the rise point of the second step with a pen. Now for the tricky bit, working across the warp width from the left to right, open the shed and throw 1½ inches of yellow, 9 inches of red and 1½ inches of yellow. Now this is simple enough, as long as you remember to loop wefts when you change colours. And so, line by line, you work the leading edge of the advancing weft until your design fits the master plan.

Note — it is most important that when you change wefts with the intention of weaving blocks of colour that have a vertical emphasis that you interlock weft passes — that is to say, you wrap wefts round each other — see working details. The weaving is continued, weft line by weft line, until the design is complete.

Once the tapestry is finished, and as described, cut it off the loom, knot-off and fringe the warp ends so that the weft is tightly contained, and then darn in any loose weft ends.

Finally, you can either sew up the sides of the bag and then lash in a plaited handle, or you can weave a narrow band (see other projects), and then sew in an integral side-panel, come handle, along the lines as illustrated.

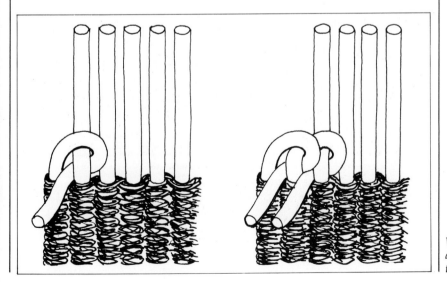

When the weaving is off the loom and clear of all strings and sticks, finish off the warp threads as shown.

AFTERTHOUGHTS AND TIPS

Although throughout this project we use the line-by-line weft building technique, Navajo rug weavers do sometimes weave and work 'hills' and 'valleys'.

If you fail to cross wefts at vertical colour change areas, your weaving will have warp slots — these can be darned over.
With a weaving of this character, go for bold contrasting colours and vigorous motifs — don't try for fiddly details.

There are other ways of linking areas of changing weft colour, see Data section. If you do decide to build you own frame loom, choose straight grained knot-free pine, and joint, glue and screw the corners.

AMERICAN FOLK ART RAG RUG

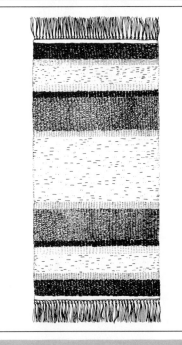

LOOM TYPE · A ROLLER FRAME LOOM WITH A RIGID HEDDLE

TECHNIQUE · A TABBY WEAVE

Inspirational illustration. A nomadic Berber girl wearing a woollen blanket with a weft striped design.

Inspirational illustration. A Czechoslovakian table cloth detail — note the weft stripes, the yarn is linen, and the colours are red, brown and yellow.

THOUGHTS ON THE PROJECT

One of the pleasures of working a traditional rag rug of this character, is the fact that you can modify, adjust and rethink the specifications, the working method, the materials, the technique etc, to suit your own unique weaving interests and design inclinations. For example, you might know something of say rag rugs, as woven by the nineteenth century Scandinavian folk weavers, in which case you might choose to work a bold colour inlay rug, on a full size floor loom. And then again, like us, you might be interested in the pioneer and folk weavings of the New World, in which case you would perhaps be aiming to save scraps of worn out garments and then weave a stout floor rug.

However, that apart, we have chosen to work this project in the early American folk style. When the settlers left their European homelands to build new lives in the American wilderness, they lived at first in wagons and rough huts. Of course it wasn't long before these crude temporary shelters were replaced by more comfortable well furnished homesteads. I see in my mind's eye poor settlers, English, Swedish, Polish, German and the like, all not being able to afford expensive imported goods, and having to improvise. Winters were cold, and fabrics were in short supply, so what to do to keep warm and beautify their homes? Simple, they saved all their old garments and recycled them to make rugs, chair covers and bedspreads. And of course, as these settlers had their roots in any number of Old World countries, so their weavings tended to be direct, naive, village-made copies of different back-home styles.

However, over the years all these different weaving styles, designs and methods, have come together and developed into what we now describe as being, 'country-rustic', 'primitive', or even 'kitchen hearth' weaving. Flip through any American 'home and gardens' type magazine, and you will be sure to see page-upon-page of traditional interiors, all with the most beautiful woven rag rugs. North American, 'primitive' rugs, folksy New

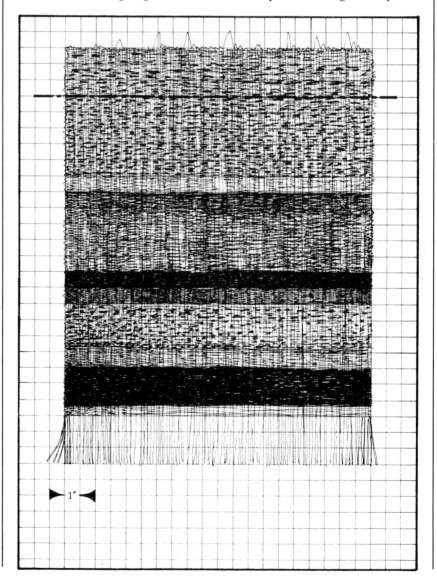

The working drawing grid, the scale is one grid square to 1 inch. See also how we have only shown half the rug.

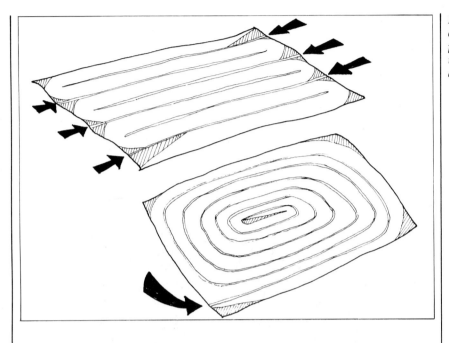

Prior to weaving and setting up the loom, collect coloured rags and cut yourself a stock- pile 1–2 inch wide weft. You can either cut the rag zig-zag fashion, or you can cut round and round.

England 'keeping room' rugs, rugs on the floors, rugs on the walls and rugs on the furniture.

Over the years, American weavers have moved away from the thrifty pioneer, make-do-and-mend approach, so much so that many weavers now use new 'off the roll' fabrics, and even work from pre-packaged kits. Modern American folk rag rugs are characterised by being tabby woven on a cotton warp, and by having well defined bands of weft colour.

CONSIDERING THE PROJECT

If you have a look at our working drawings and at our project introduction illustrations, you will see that although we are weaving a straight forward rag rug in the folk American style, we nevertheless draw our inspiration from Old World, folk and tribal weavings. Of course the Berber blanket and the Czechoslovakian table cloth are totally different in technique and concept to modern rag rugs, however that apart, we feel that their bold weft striped patterns and vigorous designs are truly inspirational. Note, that our finished rug is about 20–22 inches wide and 40 inches long.

You might choose to weave a much longer length, or even to rework the project on a loom with cord loop heddles — our considered advice is for you to shape this project to suit your own needs. As for the cut rag weft, you can use old worsted suiting, cotton sheeting, woollens, stockinette, velvet or whatever; simply start by having in mind a colour/design plan, then search around for fabrics to fit into your scheme of things.

As to the weight of weft, meaning how wide the cut rag strips need to be in relationship to the actual substance of the fabrics, the wool, the cotton, or such like, we feel that this is something you can only judge when you have

Weaver and roller frame loom, the arrangement of the roller beams, the rigid heddle and the heddle carrier.

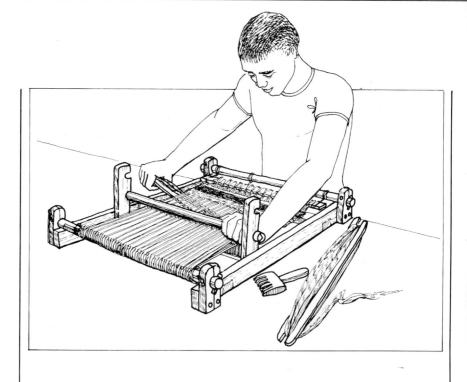

woven an inch or so of rug. We reckon to cut strips that are 1–2 inches wide according to material thickness.

Before you actually start weaving, run you own mini survey, and see if you can get some idea as to the best source of rags and their likely weight and colour.

Finally, sit back with your weft rag samples, a pack of felt tip colours and a sketch pad, and draw up a full size layout.

MATERIALS

For this project, that is weaving a 20–22 inch wide rug on a 24 inch wide roller frame loom, and allowing for eight warps to the inch, a warp length of 64 inches, doubled up selvedge warps, and a loss in warp width of about 2 inches, we estimate that you will need a 1000 feet of cabled cotton 9's single 15 ply yarn. Note — this amount of cotton yarn allows for loom wastage, weaving take-up, and for an inch or so of 'starter' and 'finish' weft. As for the amount of rags, who can say? Simply choose a type, weight and colour to suit, and then prepare a stockpile of clean cut rags as illustrated. See also our rag colour guide.

TOOLS AND EQUIPMENT

For this project you need, a roller frame table loom that measures about 24 inches wide and 36 inches long, (a loom that has front and back roller beams and a rigid heddle). You also need a tenterhook or temple, a raddle to suit the loom, a handful of shuttle sticks, a threading hook, a warping frame, a weighted claw beater, scissors, pencils, workout paper, felt tip colours and a measure.

DESIGNING AND WEFT PREPARATION

Okay then, so you have collected together your clean old rags, and you have sorted them into colour groupings. Now unpick all the seams, and cut away all lumps, bumps, buttons and raggy edges. This done, take your first piece of rag, trim off any corners, then, starting from an outside edge, cut a round-and-round strip that is about 1–2 inches wide. Work gradually towards the centre of the cloth until you have one continuous taper-ended paring, as illustrated. Now either roll the rags into balls, or better still load them onto stick shuttles.

PREPARING THE WARP

First note the total length of the warp, in this case being 64 inches. Now set up the warping frame, and using a 64 inch length of cord for a guide, arrange the pegs so that there is a three-peg cross at each end of the warp. This done, take your cabled cotton warp yarn, tie in on to one of the pegs at the end of the warp guide, then run it figure-of-eight fashion through the frame. And so you continue, running the yarn backwards and forwards through the frame until a 90 thread half-warp is well set up and established.

Now cut yourself a dozen or so lengths of cotton cord, and tie up the half-warp so that the arms of both crosses are secured. Repeat this for the other half-warp.

PUTTING THE WARP ON THE LOOM

Place the loom on your worksurface, carefully arrange the tied up warps, and then set out all your tools and materials so that they are at hand. Now there's

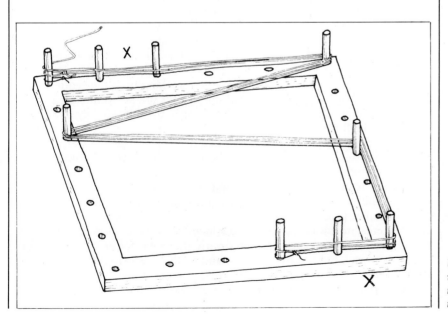

Use a guide cord set to the length of the warp, arrange the frame so that there are two 'three-peg' crosses, then take the yarn through frame and build the warp.

*Secure the warp 'crosses', as with other
projects, then take the warp off the frame,
push a shed stick through the 'cross', and
then tie the stick to the back roller beam —
that is to say the warp beam.*

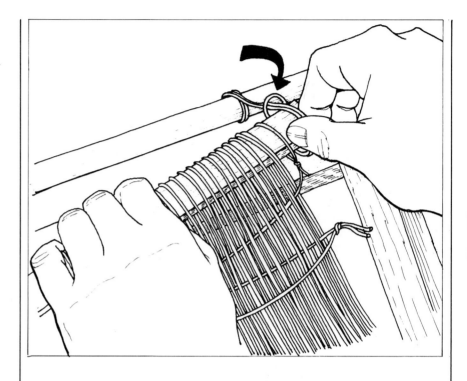

no saying that this next stage isn't difficult, so be wary and be prepared to
double check your progress.

First take a shed stick and pass it through the loop at one end of the total
warp. Now take a length of cord, run it through the other side of the cross,
and then tie it to the ends of the shed stick. You should now have one end of
the warp held secure. This done, take the secured warp end, stick, string and
all, and tie it onto the back roller beam, as illustrated.

Now place the raddle across the back of the loom, drape the warp across
the raddle, and then loosely tie it to the front roller beam. Next, cut the cross
ties from the secured end of the warp, then working from the centre of the
raddle, spread the half-warps so that the threads are set to the full 22 inch
rug width. When you reckon that the warp threads are organized, as
described and illustrated, clip the top on the raddle. Now untie the warp end
from the front roller, then get a helper to grasp and tension the warp; slowly
turn on the back roller beam so that the warp threads are combed through
the raddle and wound on. Note — to help stop warp threads sticking at a
later stage, feed sheets of newspaper onto the back roller beam between
layers of warp. When you have wound on a little over half the warp length,
push a couple of shed sticks through the front cross, then clip off the ties and
ease the cross towards the back of the loom. This done, mark the centre of
the rigid heddle with a tag of coloured yarn, then tie it across the loom width
— that is to say, tie it to the heddle stand so that it's placed about halfway
between the front roller and the back roller.

Now carefully remove the front cross ties, then cut the warp loops, take up
two pieces of cord and tie the two bunches of warp threads to the front of the

Working from the centre, space the threads in the raddle to the full width of the rug.

loom with a couple of larks-head knots, as illustrated. Next, starting at the centre of the heddle and working left, or right, it makes no matter, begin to thread up. Focus your attention onto the warp threads as they occur between the shed sticks at the cross, and select threads in order. Using a threading hook, pull the warp ends alternately down through the slots and eyes of the rigid heddle. Note that when you come to the selvedges, meaning the last four threads at each side of the warp, run the threads in pairs, two in a slot,

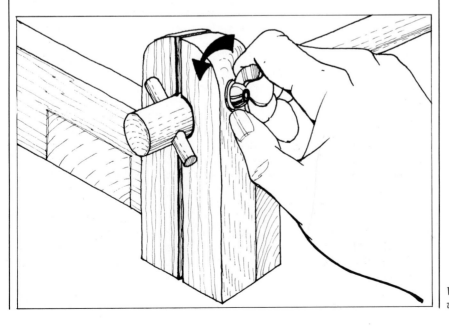

When the warp has been raddled, loosen the warp beam just prior to winding on.

Get a helper to hold and tension the warp while you wind-on the back roller.

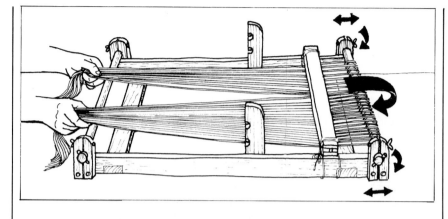

and two in an eye. And so you continue until the warp has been run alternately through eyes and slots.

Once the entering is complete, ease the rigid heddle back along the warp, and then secure it to the heddle carrier with a couple of lengths of cord. Now stroke the warp threads towards the front of the loom, and then divide them into small bundles of ten or so threads. This done, tie a shed stick to the front roller beam, then take the warp bundles (one at a time), over the stick, divide it into two, and then secure it on top with a half reef knot, as illustrated. When all the bundles have been so tied, stroke, feel and adjust the tension warp as you think fit.

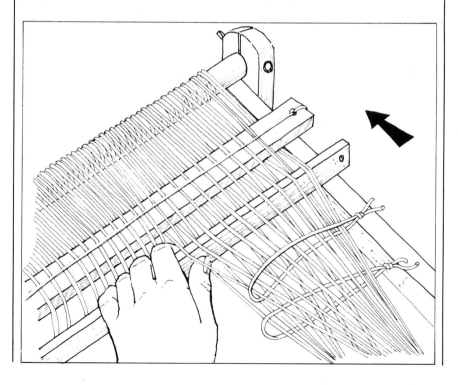

Now remove the raddle, and ease the shed sticks to the back of the loom.

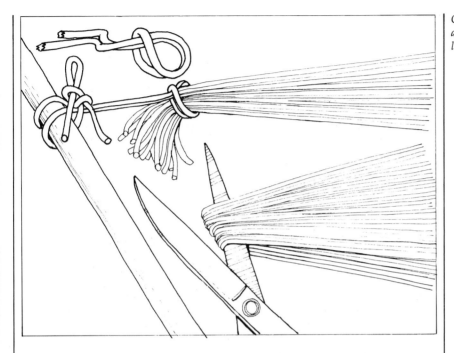

Cut the loops at the front end of the warp, and secure the two half-warps with cord and lark's-head knots.

Finally, when you judge the warp to be evenly tensioned, complete the reef knots. Note that there are a great many ways of threading up; some weavers work from the front of the loom to the back, others only use a single warp cross, and so on. How you do it isn't really important, it's the end result that counts. Our advice is to initially work as described, and then, when you

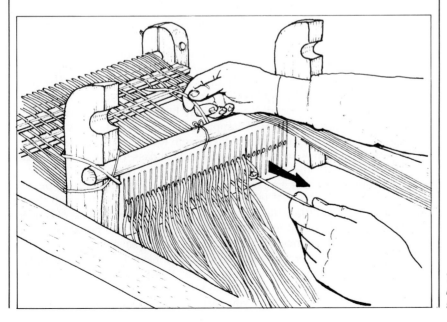

Take the warp threads in order as they occur at the 'cross', and draw them through the slots and eyes of the rigid heddle.

When all the warp threads have been drawn through the heddle, stroke them to the front of the loom, divide them into small groups, and secure them to the front roller beam with reef knots.

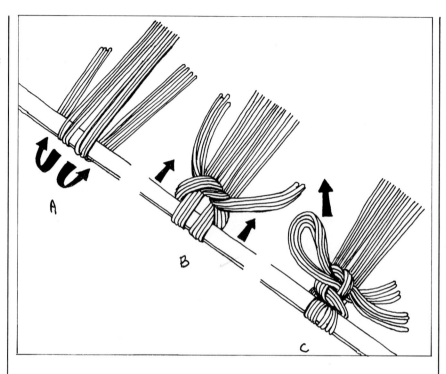

have more experience, to adjust our methods to suit your individual needs. See also our Data section and other projects.

WEAVING

When you have checked and double checked that all is correct, and as described, then clear away the clutter and organise the various cut weft strips. Start by untying the rigid heddle, then lift and lower it in its carrier, and see how the sheds work. This done, enter a couple of passes of cotton weft and have a really close-up look at the weaving structure. Make sure that you haven't say threaded neighbouring warp threads through the same slot, or missed out an eyelet thread. When you are happy that all is as described, aim to weave ½ inch or so of well compacted cotton yarn starter weft. Now have a look at your design sheet and then begin to enter the cut rag weft.

The weaving action is, up with the rigid heddle, pass the rag weft through the shed, down with the heddle, beat back with the claw beater, pass the weft back through what is now the new shed, up with the heddle, and finally beat back. Note that the weft won't cover completely — the warp will show through the weft as little white flicks. When you come to the end of a weft strip, and you want to join in a new length, simply trim and taper both new and old weft ends, then overlap about 2 inches, and weave on.

As the weaving is progressing, so you will have to use the temple/tenterhook to maintain a constant rug width. You just set the teeth of the tenterhook in the selvedges of the rug, and then lock the two wooden bars to the required width. Of course as you weave, so you will have to reposition

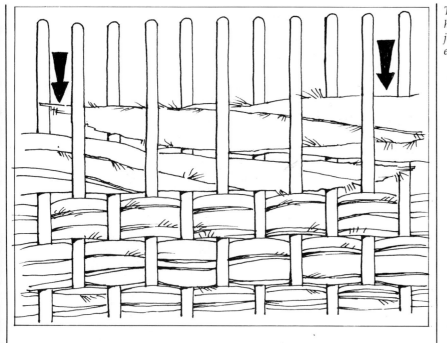

The two sheds are formed by having the rigid heddle either up or down. When you come to joining in a new length of rag weft, taper the ends and over-lap them in the same shed.

from time to time the tenterhook and wind the rug on to the front roller beam.

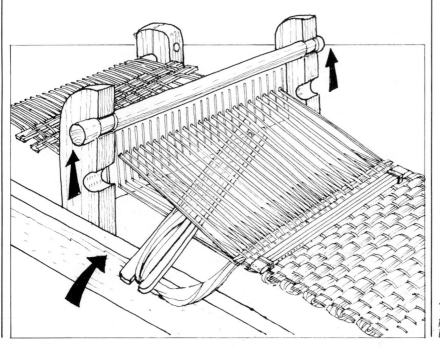

The weaving action is, up with the heddle, pass the weft through the shed, and beat back.

The second shed is achieved by having the heddle in the 'down' position.

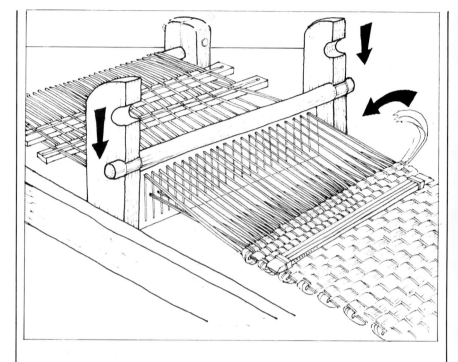

FINISHING

When you have woven the 40 inch length, or when the warp sheds are becoming restricted, finish off with $\frac{1}{2}$ inch of cotton cord weft, then, leaving the warp fringes as long as possible, free the rug from all rollers, sticks and strings. Now divide the warp ends into pairs, and knot off and fringe them so that the weft is tightly contained. Finally, turn the rug over, trim off any hanging over generous weft ends, and the job is done.

AFTERTHOUGHTS AND TIPS

If you are going to buy a new roller beam loom, choose one that has three or four heddle notches; this makes for easy weaving, and allows for a neutral 'between shed' placing and it's less strain on the warp.

Before you start weaving, or when you are buying a heddle, check that for the eight warps to the inch in this project, the heddle has four slots and four eyes to the inch. Also make sure that your chosen yarn fits the heddle.

Between weaving sessions, always slacken off the warp.

When you are throwing across the weft, arc and arch it, then you won't pull and waist the rug width.

AFRICAN STRIP CLOTH BANNER

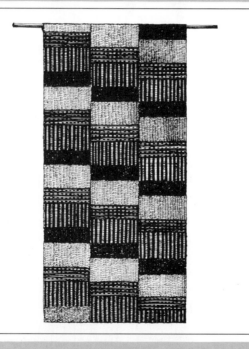

LOOM TYPE · A 4 SHAFT TABLE LOOM, WITH BACK AND FRONT ROLLER-BEAMS, WIRE HEDDLES AND AN 8 DENT REED SUPPORTED IN AN UNDERSLUNG BATTEN FRAME

TECHNIQUE · A TAPESTRY STRIP CLOTH WEAVE IN THE WEST AFRICAN TRIBAL TRADITION

Inspirational illustration. A Nigerian family wearing traditional strip-cloth togas/robes.

THOUGHTS ON THE PROJECT

In many West African tribal societies there is a tradition of weaving narrow strips of cloth. These strips might be anything from 2–16 inches in width, and they are made with the pre-conceived intention that, when woven, they be sewn together edge-to-edge to form a larger piece of cloth. These strips are rarely thought of as being weavings in their own right, that is to say as belts, braids and the like, but rather they are considered to be the raw material from which various garments are made — capes, blankets and robes. This being the case, why weave narrow strips in the first place? why not build larger looms and make wider cloths? Well, traditionally West African weavers were itinerant craftsmen, travelling from village to village weaving and working to order. This being so, they needed small portable looms.

When we were students and first researching African strip weaves, we went to a museum and asked to see examples of West African looms. Imagine our surprise when we were shown a series of dusty shoe boxes, all of which contained little stick-and-string bundles and were labelled 'West African Looms'. Weaned on vast European four poster looms, we could hardly believe our eyes — was this it? were there bits missing? where were the huge beams, the massive wooden structures and the complex webs of

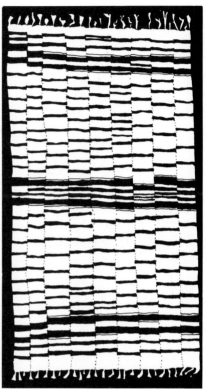

Inspirational illustration. A simple strip cloth as woven in the Upper Volta region,. The cloth is woven as a continuous strip, then the strip is cut and sewn edge to edge to make the finished cloth. Of course to make a cloth of this character, the weaver would have to have a pre-conceived notion of the finished design.

Inspirational illustration. A beautiful Adanudo strip cloth, the animal and figure motifs run in the direction of the warp.

cordage? Well, of course, when we eventually got to grips with the subject, we realised that those musty stick-and-string bundles were in fact quite sophisticated portable loom cores — that is to say, they were miniaturised reeds, heddles and pulleys. Apparently when the itinerant African weaver wanted to set up shop, he just hung his portable loom from a convenient tree, or built a stout tripod, and then to work. So where were all the wind-on beams and ratchets that we are all used to seeing? Well, after further study, we found that the front roller, or cloth beam, was either fixed directly to the weaver's waist, rather like a back-strap loom, or it was supported on a couple of forked sticks. As to the back roller-beam, this didn't exist as such; instead it was replaced by a massive sledge or dragstone, with the weight and friction of the heavy stone tensioning the warp. So there you have it, a traditional West African loom is a beautifully thought out piece of portable equipment. Of course, the one problem with a loom of this character is the fact that it is only really suitable for weaving narrow cloth widths. And so we have come in a full circle — narrow cloths were/are not woven by choice, but rather they have evolved as the logical result of loom design.

As to the structure and patterning of these narrow cloths, these vary from area to area. Yoruba weavers favour weft striped designs, the Ashanti weave and work complex twill inlays, the Mali weave tapestry inlays, and so we could go on, mentioning all manner of strip cloth types as woven by various African tribes. Finally, don't think that these African cloths are in any way crude, limited or basic, because this is certainly not the case; the weaves are sophisticated, the fabrics are of a very high quality, and the weavers use the full range of yarns, cotton, silk, wool and synthetics. And as for specific weaves from tribe to tribe, strip cloths might have warp and weft stripes, tie-and-dye patterns, warp ikat designs, tapestry weaves, printed motifs, embroidery, inlay, applique embroidery, and so I could continue, adinfinitum. From a craft weaver's point of view, West African strip cloths range from the beautiful through to the delicate and intricate — they are amazing!

CONSIDERING THE PROJECT

Have a look at our various working drawings, details and inspirational illustrations, and see how the edge-to-edge placing of the strips, perhaps more than anything else, makes a cloth exciting. In themselves the woven strips are, more often than not, simply repeats of rather basic woven passages, perhaps a weft line, a few warp lines, another weft line and so on; but cut the strips into sections, place them edge-to-edge and then stagger the woven blocks of colour, and immediately the made-up cloths become exotic, vibrant and dynamic.

So with this project, it is most important that you start by having a well-formed idea of just how the strips of pattern look when they are set side by side. Maybe you could work your initial designs with cut coloured paper. When you are designing, don't aim to have precise blocks of colour, much better to build into the strips a slight mis-alignment factor. Try not to be too rigid or follow our measurements slavishly, but rather just aim to work a module that has about it an element of unpredictability. For example, if you look at the Upper Volta cloth, as illustrated, you will see that although each

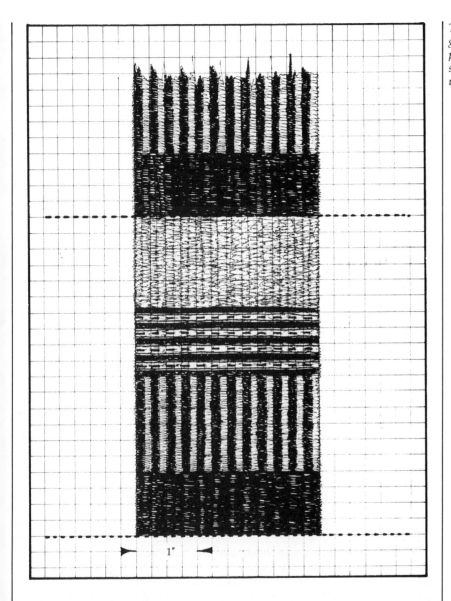

The working grid. Note the grid scale of four grid squares to 1 inch, and see also the possible colour arrangement (we only show a single block, this has to be repeated to make up the total cloth).

strip length does have the same number of black and white bands, nevertheless the weaver has consciously varied the visual weight of the bands so that subtle mis-alignment has been achieved.

In this project we suggest that you work an approximately 5 inch band of pattern, as described, and that you repeat this 5 inch band the full length of the strip. See how we have tried to pre-design the 5 inch repeat so that the end result can be staggered in a variety of ways. Of course when you work the strip, by its very nature the woven repeats will vary in size, tone and structure; in this project, these variations are to be encouraged. Our woven strip, as described and illustrated, is 3 inches wide and about 65 inches long,

The loom — we use a 4 shaft table loom, one with wire heddles.

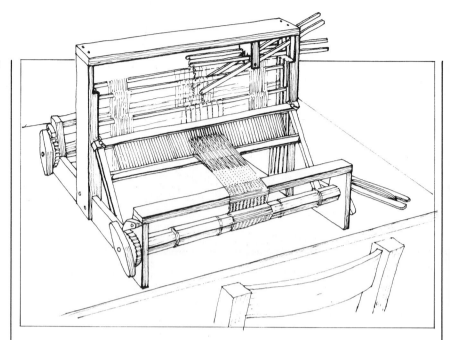

that is to say, it is made up of thirteen 5 inch repeats. If you look at the working drawings you will see that the banner is made up of three staggered strips that are sewn edge-to-edge, so the finished banner measures about 9–10 inches wide and 19–21 inches long. See how the staggered arrangement of the three strips means that you have to weave an extra 5 inch repeat.

Now for the loom — we have chosen to weave this strip on a straightforward 4 shaft table loom, see Data section. Of course a loom of this character is outside the West African strip weaving tradition, but nevertheless we feel that the wire heddles, the arrangement of the reed and the general shape of the loom is not only right for this project, but it fits into our scheme of things.

MATERIALS

This project is tapestry weaving a 3 inch wide, 65 inch long strip, allowing for eight warp ends to the inch, a total warp length of 90 inches, doubled up warp threads at the selvedge, loom wastage, 'start' and 'finish' weft, and so on. We reckon that you will need, at least 210 feet of 9's single, 15 ply white cabled cotton for the warp, and 500–600 feet of mercerised cotton 4/10's (colour to suit) for the weft. Note — as with all the other projects, it is very difficult to say just how much weft you will need, because after all you might beat back hard, weave loose, or whatever. Our weft estimations are based on thirty wefts to the inch.

TOOLS AND EQUIPMENT

For this project you need a 4 shaft table loom — one with back and front roller-beams, wire heddles and an 8 dent reed supported in an underslung batten frame. You also need a raddle to suit the loom, a couple of stick shuttles, half a dozen shed sticks, a threading hook and a warping frame.

And of course you will also need all the usual workshop tools like scissors, pencils, workout paper, colours and a tape measure.

DESIGNING

Have a good look at our various working drawings and illustrations and see how we have used the 5 inch strip repeat. Now either settle for the same design, or take your workout paper and play around with our arrangement and see if you can come up with a design of your own. Finally, when you have achieved a good workable design and it fits into your scheme of things, draw up a single motif to size.

PREPARING THE WARP

Note the warp length of 90 inches and now set up the warping frame using a 90 inch length of cotton for a guide. Arrange the pegs so that there is a three-peg cross at each end of the warp. Now knot-on the warp yarn to one end of the frame, as illustrated, then run it figure-of-eight fashion backwards and forwards through the frame. Aim in this instance to make a 3 inch wide warp that has a total of twenty-eight ends — this allows for eight ends to the inch, and doubled up selvedges. This done, take some short lengths of yarn, and tie up the warp so that all the crosses are stabilised and secure.

PUTTING THE WARP ON THE LOOM

Start by setting the loom on a level worksurface, then pin up all your inspirational drawings and design work, and set out your tools and materials. Now very carefully take the tied-up warp from the frame, and place it on the

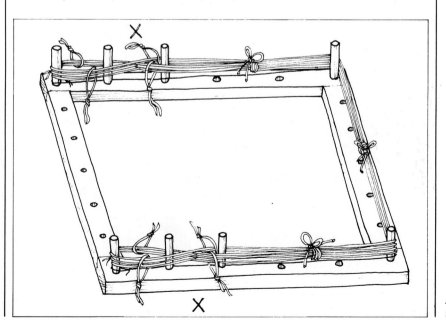

Arrange the frame so that the warp has a three-peg 'cross' at each end.

Put the two, tied and secured, half-warps through the loom, then tie the shed stick to the back roller beam. Note — this loom is viewed from the back, and it has roller cords rather than an apron.

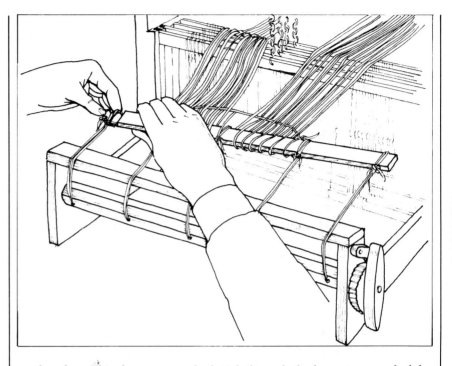

worksurface. This done, pass a shed stick through the loop at one end of the warp, then pass a cord through the other side of the cross and tie it to the ends of the shed stick. So far so good, this end of the warp can now be

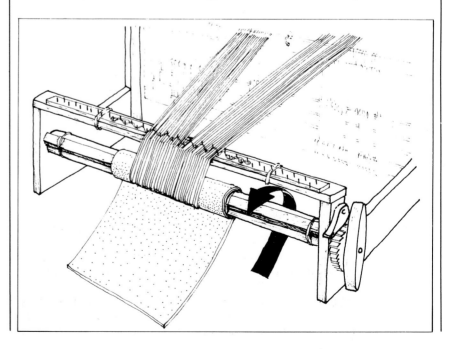

Spread the warp threads in the raddle so as to make up the cloth width, then, with a helper pulling on the warp, carefully wind the warp onto the back roller — see how between warp layers we roll on a thick card/ paper, it stops the threads from catching.

transferred to the back roller-beam of the loom and tied in place, as illustrated. Now tie the raddle across the back of the loom, then pass the warp over the raddle and very loosely tie it to the front roller-beam. This done, carefully remove the various cross-ties from the back end of the warp, and spread the warp threads in the raddle so that they are set to the 3 inch strip width.

Now for the bit where you need a helping hand — remove a few more warp ties, loose the front end of the warp from the loom, and then get your helper to grasp and tension the warp. You can now slowly wind the warp onto the back roller-beam. As the warp is being wound on, feed sheets of paper between the roller-beam and the warp layers, and at the same time check that the warp threads are being evenly combed through the teeth of the raddle. When you have wound on about two-thirds of the warp length, push a couple of shed sticks through the front cross, as illustrated. Now remove the final cross-ties and ease the cross through the loom until it's

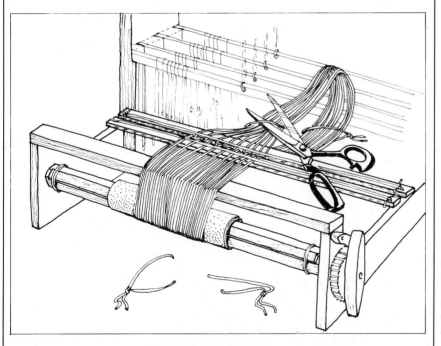

When the warp has been wound on, remove the raddle, push the two front shed sticks to the back of the loom, then very carefully remove the 'cross' ties from the front end of the warp, and secure the warp to the front roller beam with a couple of lark's-head knots.

about half way between the heddles and the back roller. This done, cut the front warp loops, divide the warp into half (14 threads in each half), then fix the two half-warps to the front corners of the loom with cords and a couple of lark's-head knots. Now find the centre-point of the heddles, and sweep them all left and right to the sides of the loom.

With masking tape and a pencil, label the four heddle-frames (shafts), from the back of the loom to the front, so that they are numbered, 1, 2, 3 and 4.

This done, focus your attention onto the warp threads as they pass through the cross, and note how they can be picked off in order. Now selecting the threads from the left-hand bundle of warps, take your threading

Draw the warp threads, in the order as described, through the eyes of the heddles — note how each little group of threads is tied off (for the sake of clarity, we haven't shown the reed).

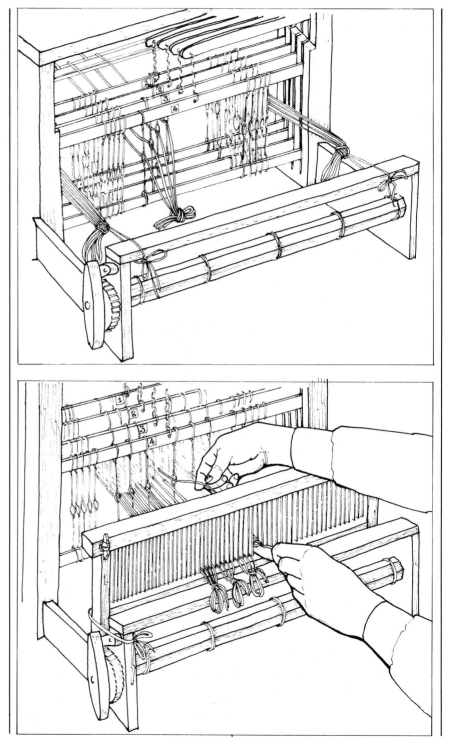

Starting at the centre of the reed, draw the threads through the slots/dents; and again tie them in groups of four.

hook and thread-up the wire heddles in the order 1, 2, 3 and 4. Repeat this threading sequence three times, but on the last 3 and 4 heddles, run threads in pairs for the selvedge. This done, work the right-hand bunch of warps in the same way, but this time work from centre to right, and thread-up the heddles in the order 4, 3, 2 and 1. Note — as each little sequence is complete, group and tie the four threads with a slip knot.

Once all the warp threads have been passed through the heddle wires, as described, then they need to be threaded through the reed. Start at the centre of the warp, as before, and enter the threads through the reed dents/slots in the same order — don't forget that at the selvedges run two threads as one. This done, stroke the warp to the front of the loom, and divide it into small bundles of 4 threads. Now tie a shed stick to the front roller-beam, and carefully divide the warp bundles and run them over the shed stick and

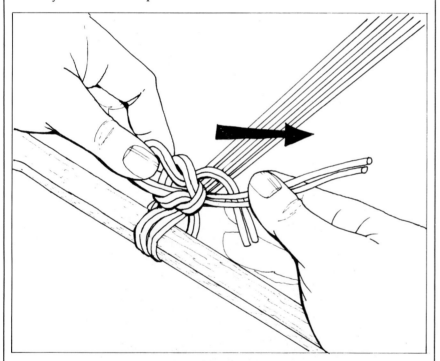

When all the warp threads have been threaded and checked, fix them to the front roller beam, as shown in other projects.

secure them, as illustrated, with a half reef knot. When all the bundles have been so tied, strum your finger tips delicately backwards and forwards over the warp web and retension the threads as you think fit. Finally, complete the other half of the reef knots and the job is done.

WEAVING

Start by checking your threading order, raise both the shafts/heddle-frames 1 and 3, and see how the warps go alternately up and down and form the first shed. Now lower 1 and 3, and raise 2 and 4, and see how the warp threads go alternately up and down for the second shed. When you are sure that all is correct, clear away all the mess and have another look at your chosen design

To test for correct and even warp tension, gently stroke your fingers over the warp. If any threads feel to be 'proud', then they need to be slackened and re-adjusted.

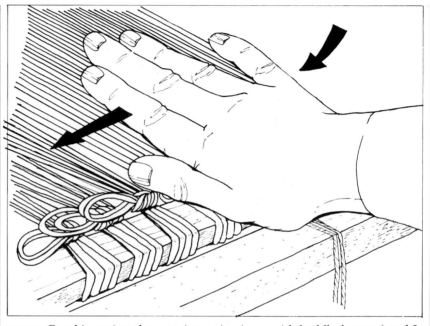

repeat. For this project the weaving action is up with heddle frames 1 and 3, pass the weft through the shed, and at one and the same time close the shed and beat back with the reed. Now up with heddle frames 2 and 4, pass the

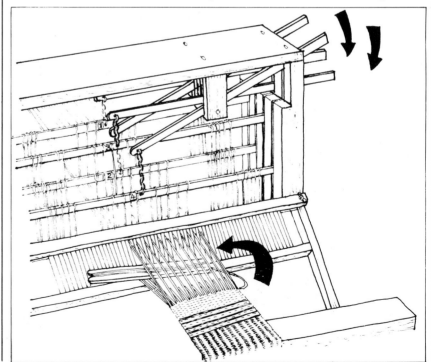

The first shed is achieved by having shafts/ harnesses 1 and 3 in the 'up' position.

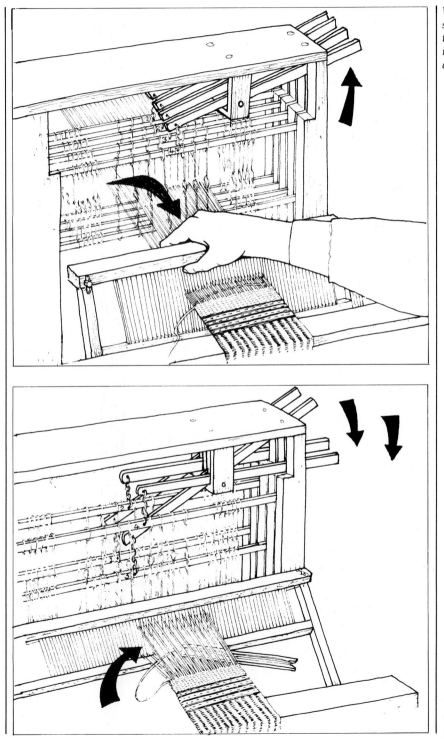

When the weft has been passed through the shed, the shed can be closed down just prior to beating back. See how the weft is arranged in a little arc, and note how in the 'closed down' position all levers are 'up' and at rest.

The second shed is achieved by having shafts/ harnesses 2 and 4 in the 'up' position.

weft through the shed and beat back. And so you continue to work through all the various passages of weft colour. Weave first an inch of dark, then 1½ inches of alternate weft colours, then an inch of light and dark weft groupings, and finally 1½ inches of plain light weft (see working details).

Once you have woven the full 5 inches, or thereabouts, then repeat the sequence until you have woven all thirteen blocks, that is to say the whole 65 inch long strip. As likely as not, when you are weaving, you will forget how many 5 inch lumps you have woven, so mark each repeat with a little tag of coloured wool. Also it might help if you pin your full-size colour design beside the warp as you are weaving.

FINISHING

When you have woven the full 65 inches of warp, weave an inch or two for good measure, then cut the whole warp from the loom and free it from all sticks and strings. Finally, turn the long woven strip over and darn in all loose weft ends.

SEWING THE BANNER CLOTH

Have a look at our designs, etc, then cut the 65 inch long strip into three lengths as shown. Now place the strips side by side, on a clean worksurface, and experiment with various staggered placings. You might even reverse the strips or turn them upside down. When you feel that you have achieved a satisfactory design, take a needle and your chosen weft colours and join the strips edge-to-edge with a running over-and-over stitch. Finally, sew the banner to a display rod, as illustrated, and give it a straight rolled and sewn hem.

AFTERTHOUGHTS AND TIPS

With this project the emphasis isn't so much on the actual weaving, but rather on the initial designing, and on the placing of the three pieces of strip once they have been woven.

If after you have woven the strip you still have some spare warp, you can experiment with various shaft and shed sequences. For example, you might run the shafts in the order, 1, 2 and 3, 4, or 1, 4 and 2, 3. With a tapestry weave of this character, the weft totally covers the warp.

Although narrow strip cloths are still being woven in West Africa, the weavers now work in settled co-operatives rather than travelling around.

GUATEMALAN BROCADED APRON

**LOOM TYPE · A 4 SHAFT TABLE LOOM, WITH BACK AND FRONT
ROLLER- BEAMS, WIRE HEDDLES AND A 10 DENT REED SUPPORTED IN AN
UNDERSLUNG BATTEN FRAME**

**TECHNIQUE · TABBY WEAVE WITH BROCADED MANUAL PICK-UP
MOTIFS**

Inspirational illustration. A Central American Indian woman wearing a characteristic traditional brocaded Huipil — note the simple pattern and cut.

THOUGHTS ON THE PROJECT

Guatemala is the largest country in Central America; in very general picture book terms, it's a land of tropical lowlands, rain forests, frozen highlands, Indians, small scattered villages, chickens and maize. However if we adjust our focus and look a little closer at our main areas of weaving interest, that is to say the poorer more isolated rural highland villages, we would see that the Indians live a well-established almost self-sufficient life-style that centres around craft skills, the cultivation of small pieces of land, market days and religious festivals.

As for weaving, traditionally the Indians wove cloth for their own use and then sold the surplus at the local markets. Now of course as most of the weavings are made for the tourists, with the weavers using for the most part imported machine spun and chemically dyed yarns, so the styles and designs have coarsened and become more obvious. However, in broad terms, I think it fair to say that the overall picture of Guatemalan weaving remains unchanged. The women weavers use two types of spindle, a drop stick whorl for alpaca and sheep wool, and a bowl supported thigh-rubbed spindle for cotton. They then take the spun yarn and make the warps directly on pegs which are banged into the ground. Finally, with minimal equipment, the warps are turned into simple back-strap looms — see Data section and the project details.

As to the actual weaves, enough to say that they are many and varied — tapestry, double-cloth, brocading, ikats, bands, inlay, etc, etc — the weavers use just about every hand weaving technique that we can think of. That apart, glorious as most of these weaves are, we feel that the most important

Inspirational illustration. A detail showing a sheep motif.

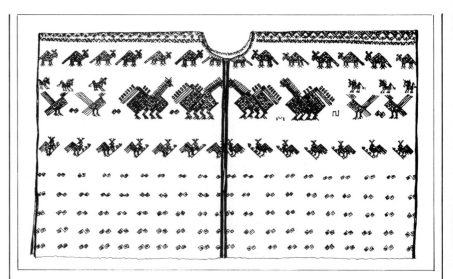

feature of Guatemalan weaving is not so much the actual weaves, but rather the fact that all the traditional clothes are made on the loom. That is to say, the loom widths are designed and decorated with the express intention that when woven they be taken off the loom and, with hardly any cutting, turned directly into garments. So, as seen on the loom, a width of cloth would be say the front of a blouse, the sides of a bag, a belt, a shawl, a sash and so on. The weaver would as it were not be just working a length of cloth, she would be weaving part of a specific item of clothing. For example, the Guatemalan blouse or huipil is made up from two or three loom widths, no complex cutting or shaping and the widths are taken from the loom and sewn directly edge-to-edge to make the garment. The advantage of working in this manner is in fact that the weaver can build decorative features into the cloth, with the certain knowledge that they will occur say across a blouse front, or along an arm slit. This whole intimate way of working has resulted in weavers, tribes and communities concentrating their weaving efforts on achieving uniquely individual motifs and designs. So the Pocaman Indians weave huipils that are brocaded with birds, deer and armadillos, the Otomi Indians weave bands and sashes that are decorated with chickens, pigeons and plants, and so on. The woven designs, from village to village, are all individualised and related to local animals, local customs and meaningful tribal symbols.

Many of the woven designs look to be and are often described as 'embroidered', but in fact they are brocaded; meaning the weaver sets the loom up for a plain or gauze cloth width, and then as she weaves, she picks up, selects warp threads and enters bulky coloured wefts to build patterns and motifs. The various designs are traditionally passed down from mother to daughter, and if compared designs are anything to go on, that is to say designs as seen on nineteenth-century weavings and on ancient pottery, it is likely that many modern woven designs have their roots in pre-Hispanic Indian cultures.

And so it is, that on modern weavings ancient pagan Mayan symbols like serpents and birds appear alongside Spanish heraldic eagles and Christian crosses. What else to say? except to emphasise the fact that weaving is such an important part of Guatemalan tribal society, that girls, before marriage, are required to demonstrate their weaving skills.

Inspirational illustration. A detail from a man's head cloth, woven by the Quiche Indians — the motif shows a 'clamorous' bird. Note how the design is made up of weft floats on a plain ground.

CONSIDERING THE PROJECT

If you look at our working drawings and details, you will see that we have chosen to work within the spirit of the Guatemalan weavers. Our apron is worked and woven on the loom and then made-up with the minimum of cutting and sewing. See how the project is woven in a medium fine cotton, how the brocaded motifs are worked with a bulky red cotton weft, and how they are made up of floated weft threads.

The cloth has a plain white tabby woven ground and we have set the loom at twenty warp ends to the inch. As for the brocading, for the most part, this can be managed by raising single selected heddle frames, (shafts), but when you come to the motif details, you will not only have to raise single shafts, you will also have to further select and reject warp threads manually. We have chosen to build the little motifs using weft floats — have a close look at

The working drawing grid — note the two grid scales, the top one is at five grid squares to ¹/₂ inch, and the bottom one is at two grid squares to ¹/₂ inch.

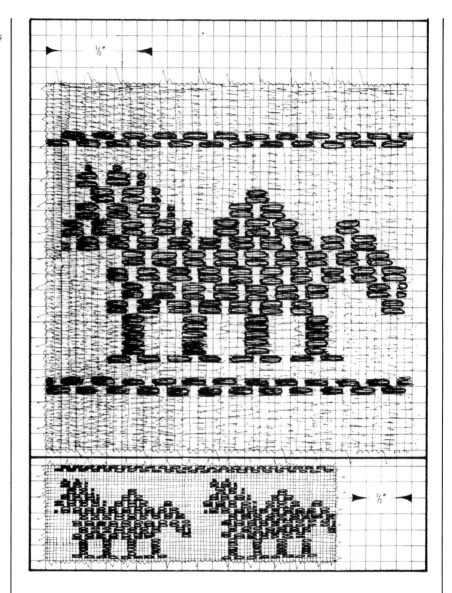

the working details, and see how the wefts skip and float over three warps. Now for the loom — yes you could work this project using a traditional Guatemalan backstrap loom, and it would certainly be an enlightening and valuable craft experience, however, in this instance, we have chosen to use a 4 shaft table loom with wire heddles and a 10 dent reed beater.

Now before you go much further, try if possible to take a trip to an ethnic museum, and get to see examples of Guatemalan, Mexican and Peruvian weaving. Take a sketch pad, and study the various patterns, designs and motifs. Note — in England the best collection of such weavings is, The

McDougall Collection of Indian Textiles from Guatemala, in the Pitt Rivers Museum, Oxford.

When you feel that you understand just how Indian brocades are put together, you might also stop and consider whether or not you want to weave traditional motifs, or say change the designs and have maybe a name, a personalised pattern or some such. However, if you do decide to modify our project, make sure your workouts are well considered and gridded up. Finally, just prior to weaving draw out the brocaded motifs to size.

MATERIALS

For this project, that is tabby weaving a 22 inch wide, 34 inch long cotton cloth with brocaded motifs and allowing for twenty ends to the inch (for both warp and weft) a total warp length of 58 inches, and all the usual selvedges and loom wastage extras, we have calculated that you will need about 4000 feet of white mercerised 4/10's cotton. As for the brocading, meaning the weft floats, we have chosen to work them all in red 4/10's cotton. You might want to use up spare yarn from another project or work all the motifs in different colours, no matter, we reckon that you will need about 60 feet of yarn. Note — if you want to make this woven length into an apron, you will need 10 feet of $\frac{1}{2}$ inch cotton tape.

TOOLS AND EQUIPMENT

For this project you will need a 4 shaft table loom, ideally one with back and front roller-beams, wire heddles and a 10 dent reed supported in an underslung batten. You will also need a raddle to suit the loom, wire toothed or wood pegged it makes no matter, a couple of stick shuttles for the brocade weft, a boat shuttle for the tabby weft, a threading hook, a reed hook, a tenterhook, a selection of shed sticks, and last but not least a warping frame. Finally, don't forget you will need a whole heap of other tools and materials like scissors, pencils, workout paper, colours and a tape measure.

Note — as we are working the three brocaded motifs with a single colour, and don't mind having very long floats at the back of the cloth, we are carrying the red cotton on stick shuttles. However, if you decide to work the motifs all in different colours, you will need to use individual tapestry type bobbins rather than shuttles (see Data section).

PREPARING THE WARP

Set out the warping frame pegs with a guide cotton warp length of 58 inches, and arrange the pegs so that there is a three-peg cross at each end of the warp. Now before you go any further, note that at twenty ends to the inch, a warp width of 22 inches, and allowing for extra selvedge threads, there are a total of 448 threads — that is to say, two half-warps each with 224 threads. Once

Making the warp, use the guide cord to set the length of the warp, then build a warp that has a three-peg 'cross' at each end. Before you remove the warp from the frame, make sure that it's secure and well tied.

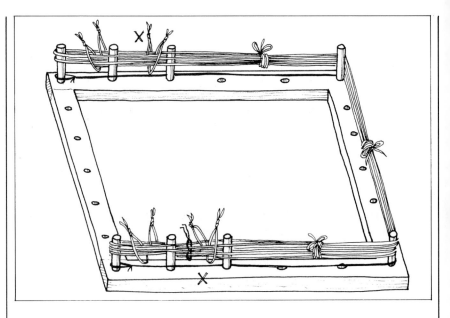

you have established the warp length, etc, run your cotton warp yarn through the frame and make two tied and secured half-warps, as already described in other projects. Note — look at the illustration details and see how we have used a coloured in-and-out thread at the cross, this saves you having to recount the threads.

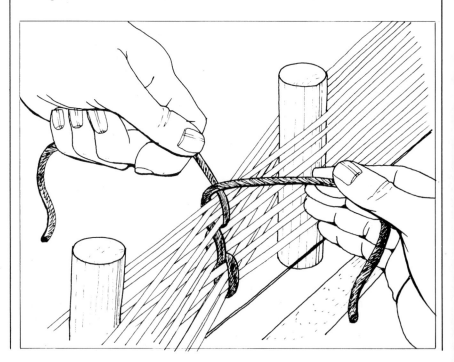

When you are making the warp, you might loop in a length of coloured yarn at the 'cross', this divides the warp threads into groups, and makes for easy counting and checking.

PUTTING THE WARP ON THE LOOM

This warp is certainly more difficult to put on the loom than say the last project, but only because you are dealing with a finer yarn, and a greater number of warp ends. This being the case, all the more reason for having your wits about you and working quietly through all the mind calming business of arranging your working area and setting out all your tools and materials. When you are sure that the two half-warp skeins are well established and tied, then pass a shed stick through the loop at one end of the warp, pass a cord the other side of the cross, and then knot the ends of the cord to the ends of the stick. Next set the raddle across the back of the loom, and cover its teeth with folded paper, as illustrated. Now tie the secure end of the warp, meaning the end with the shed stick, to the back roller-beam, and pass the other end of the warp over the raddle, through the loom

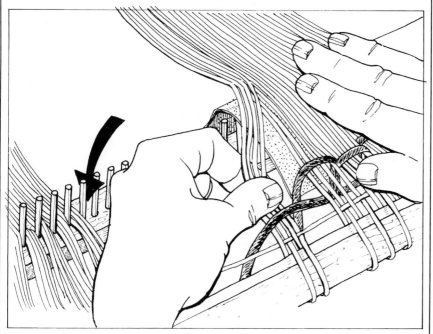

Tie the shed stick to the back roller beam, rest the warp on the raddle card, then set the warp threads in the raddle so that they fill out the cloth width.

and loosely tie it to the front roller. Starting at the centre of the raddle, carefully space the warps so that they are set the full 22 inch cloth width, and clip on the raddle top. Note — if you have any doubts as to the raddle top being well fixed, tie the cover strip on with a couple of lengths of cord.

Now get your helper to unlock the front of the warp. This done, your helper can pull on, and tension the warp, while you roll the other end onto the back roller-beam. As the warp is being wound on and combed through the raddle, so you can feed some stout paper, or shed sticks, between the back roller and the warp layers. When you have wound on about half the warp length, push two shed sticks through the front warp cross, then remove the warp ties and gently ease the cross towards the back of the loom. This done, gather all the wire heddles so that they are grouped at the centre

When the warp has been spaced in the raddle, clip and tie on the cover strip. Now get a helper to pull and tension the warp, while you wind it on to the back roller beam. See how shed sticks are placed between warp layers.

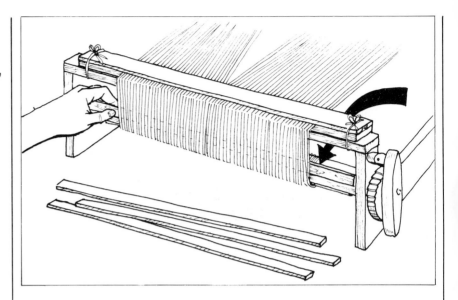

of the loom, then cut all the front warp loops and take the two half-warps forward (one each side of the loom) so that they are between the heddles and the sides of the loom. Now fix the two half-warps to the front corners of the loom with a couple of lark's-head knots, as illustrated. Next find the centre points on all four heddle frames, then sweep all the heddles left and right, so that they are hard up against the sides of the loom and the secured warp.

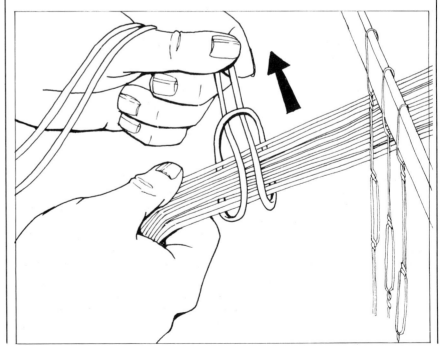

Take the half-warps through the loom between the loom sides and the heddle wires, and fix them to the front of the loom with a couple of lark's head knots. Finally, complete the loom threading etc, as shown and described in other projects.

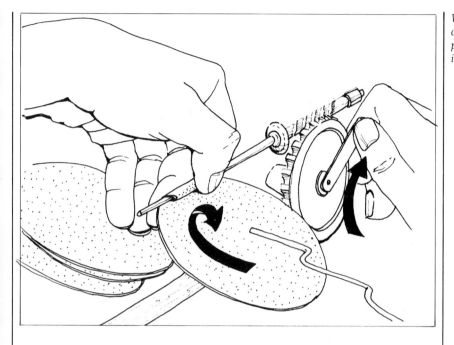

When you come to winding your weft yarn onto bobbins, roll paper 'quills' onto the prong of the winder, let the yarn get drawn in, then continue to wind.

Now with masking tape and pencil, label the four heddle frames (shafts) from the back of the loom to the front, so that they are numbered 1, 2, 3 and 4.

Now clear away all the clutter and be ready with the threading hook. Starting on the left-hand side of the loom, select warp threads in order as they occur at the cross, that is to say as they occur between the two shed sticks. Thread up the wire heddles in the order 1, 2, 3 and 4. As you work each little four-thread group, secure the four threads with a slip knot, double check the sequence, then go on to the next group. And so you continue, until you have threaded up all the 224 threads of the left-hand half-warp. Note — don't forget to double up the last four threads so that they run through two heddle wires and strengthen the selvedge. And of course you work the right-hand half-warp in like manner, but this time thread up in the heddle frame order 4, 3, 2 and 1.

When you have checked and rechecked that all is correct, put the reed in its frame, find its centre, then starting at the centre of the reed start to pass, or sley, the warps through the reed dents/slots. Note as there are twenty warp ends to the inch, and only 10 reed dents to the inch, you need to enter two warps through each slot of the reed.

Of course as you work the warp threads through the reed, again check the order and tie the groups with slip knots. This done, tie a shed stick to the front roller-beam and stroke the total warp to the front of the loom. Now gather little bundles of threads, divide each bundle and carefully take it over the shed stick and secure it with a half reef knot. Do this with the whole warp, as illustrated in other projects. Finally, run your finger tips gently backwards and forwards over the warp, adjust the tension as you think fit, and then complete the reef knots.

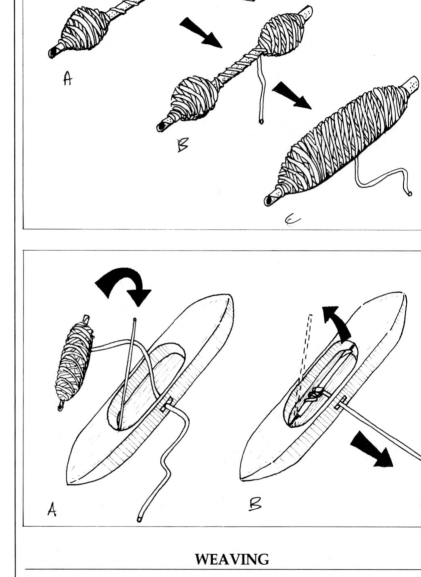

Build up the bobbins in the order, as shown, that is to say, build up at the quill ends and then fill in to make a plump sausage .

Loading a shuttle. (A) make sure that the bobbin fits the shuttle, then pass the yarn end through the 'feed' eye, place the bobbin on the rod, and finally clip the rod in position. (B) when the shuttle is almost empty, remove the quill, take out any fluff, and then reload.

WEAVING

First check the threading order and the loom operation. Raise the heddle frames/shafts in pairs, start with 1 and 3 — the shed needs to be clear and the warps should be placed alternately up and down. You might pass a large coloured trial weft through the shed. Now lower heddle frames 1 and 3, and raise 2 and 4, and check in this way. This done, load your boat shuttle with white weft thread and off you go.

When you come to passing or throwing the shuttle through the shed, sit the shuttle on the batten race and give it a flick with your wrist and index finger. Note — as you are throwing the shuttle backwards and forwards through the shed, make sure that the shuttle eyelet is facing you.

The background tabby weaving is simple and straightforward, the action is up with heddle frames 1 and 3, pass the weft through the shed, close the shed and beat back. Now up with heddle frames 2 and 4, pass the weft through the shed and again close down and beat back. And so you continue

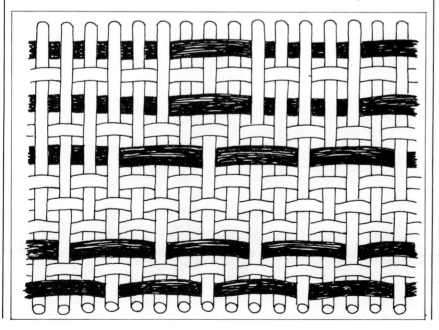

Throughout this project, that is to say when you are weaving the ground cloth and also when you are working the brocaded design, you must continue to weave the background tabby. You must make sure that the tabby sequence, before and after a throw of decorative weft, is constant.

When you are weaving, lay in in little tag of
coloured yarn every 4–6 inches, then, even
when the woven cloth is wound round the
front roller beam, you will be able to tell at a
glance just how much cloth you have woven.

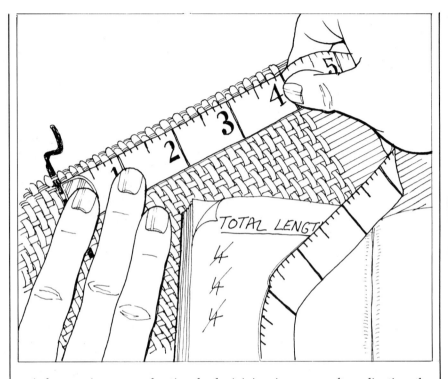

quietly weaving away, beating back, joining in new wefts, adjusting the
selvedge, etc, until you have woven about 6 inches of plain white tabby.
     When you have reached this stage, stop weaving, and try raising a single

The weft pick-up design is achieved by hand
selected warp threads.

heddle frame/shaft, say . . . number 1. See how when you have one shaft up, this gives you a shed sequence of one thread up and three threads down, one thread up and three threads down, and so on the full warp width. Now take your red weft, pass it through this new shed, and then close down and beat back. This done, have a long look at the weaving order and see how the red weft floats, or skips, over three warps and under one. Now weave another line of tabby weft. Next repeat the red three-float pass, but this time raise heddle frame 3, and beat back. You should now have a two-line stripe of three-float staggered red weft, rather like a brick wall pattern (see details). When you are sure that all is correct and as described, put down the red weft, take up the white, and continue weaving the plain tabby as before. Note — if you look at the working drawings and details, you will see that there are four staggered stripe lines in all — a total of eight, warp-width, passes of red weft.

WORKING THE BROCADED MOTIFS

Continue weaving a plain white tabby background patterned with red weft stripes, as illustrated in our working drawings. When you have woven about $28\frac{1}{2}$ inches of warp, that is to say you have woven the third red stripe and about $\frac{1}{4}$ inch of white tabby, then you can start working the brocaded horse motifs.

Have a good look at our details, and see how, for the most part, the motifs are made up of various arrangements of red weft floats that skip over three warps. The weaving order in broad terms is a throw of tabby, a throw of brocade, a throw of tabby, and so on. However the motif details are made by rejecting and selecting individual warp threads. This being the case, when you come to weaving the motifs you can certainly raise single heddle frames/

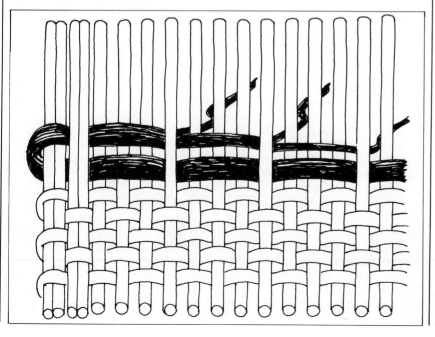

When you want to join in a new length of coloured weft, stagger the ply strands, double back round the selvedge warp thread, and overlap for about an inch.

shafts so that three-float sheds are open, but nevertheless there will come a time when you will have to use a stick shuttle or tapestry bobbins to pick and select individual warps. Of course initially you will no doubt stumble and make mistakes, but no matter, you won't go far wrong as long as you remember all the while to keep the background tabby weave constant and well organised.

FINISHING AND MAKING UP THE APRON

When you have woven the full 34 inches of the warp, cut it off the loom and free it from all sticks and strings. This done, take a needle, flip the weaving over so that it's face down, then darn in all loose weft ends. Now carefully roll, pin and sew both ends of the weaving, so that you have a finished cloth

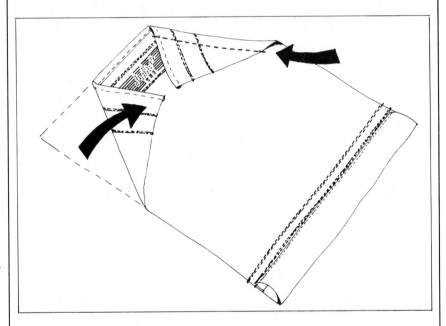

To make the apron place the woven cloth face down, hem top and bottom edges, then fold back and sew the top corners to make the tape 'pockets'.

length of about 28–29 inches. This done have a look at the constructional details — no cutting or fitting, you just fold back and sew the two top corners so that the brocaded motifs are nicely arranged, then you thread the 10 foot tape through the sewn flaps and the job is done.

AFTERTHOUGHTS AND TIPS

When you are building the warp and joining in new lengths of yarn, always tie a good, secure non-slip knot, and make sure it is placed at one end or other of the warp.

This project isn't more complex than the others, however there are certainly a great many more warp ends — this being the case, you will have to make doubly sure that the warp is well tied before you take it from the warping frame.

A modern Peruvian hanging dated about 1920 — note the heavy tapestry weave, and the use of ancient pre-Spanish motifs.

When you have finished threading up the first half-warp in the order 1, 2, 3 and 4, and you are about to start on the second half-warp, it is vital that you remember to reverse the sequence and work the heddle frames in the order 4, 3, 2 and 1 — always check and double check.

If you want to work the three horses in three different colours, or you want to work them in the same colour, but don't want to have huge weft floats at the back of the fabric, then you can weave the motifs individually and carry the weft on three different bobbins. If you do decide to work in this way, then the brocade weft turns will occur at the motif edges.

When you throw the red weft stripes, and it's good weaving practice to double back the weft ends at the selvedges, it makes for a secure, tidy finish.

Although we have mentioned a tenterhook in the tools list, you might or might not have to use one, see how it goes.

A Kachlin bag, North India. This bag was woven and made in two pieces. The yarn is cotton, and the pattern is achieved by having a weft-faced brocade, and a tapestry weave.

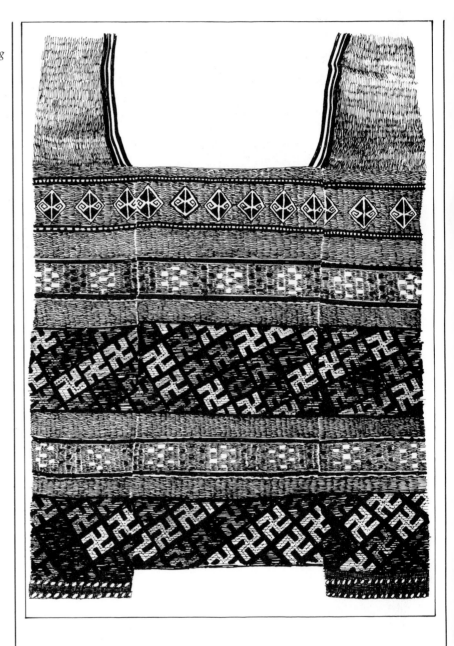

EUROPEAN FOLK-WEAVE BEDSPREAD

LOOM TYPE · A FOOT-POWERED TRADITIONAL EUROPEAN/DANISH TYPE FLOOR LOOM WITH BACK AND FRONT ROLLER-BEAMS, A RISING SHED ACTION, 4 SHAFTS, STRING HEDDLES, 4 JACKS, AND 6 PEDALS

TECHNIQUE · A PLAIN TABBY WEAVE, PLUS A MONK'S BELT WEAVE CENTRAL PANEL

Inspirational illustration. A young
Czechoslovakian woman wearing items of
traditional dress — a handwoven blouse and
apron.

THOUGHTS ON THE PROJECT

All over Europe weaving gradually evolved from its primitive beginnings to become a vital and important craft. Of course, from country to country, the emphasis of the craft varied, with weavers concentrating on different distinctive fabrics — woollens in England, linen in Czechoslavakia, silk, velvet and so on. In broad general terms, the overall development of European weaving was the same; as soon as individual weaving communities had established their specific areas of craft knowledge, so they tended to protect their craft with complex 'closed shops' and guilds. Over the five hundred year period beginning around 1400, weaving became more

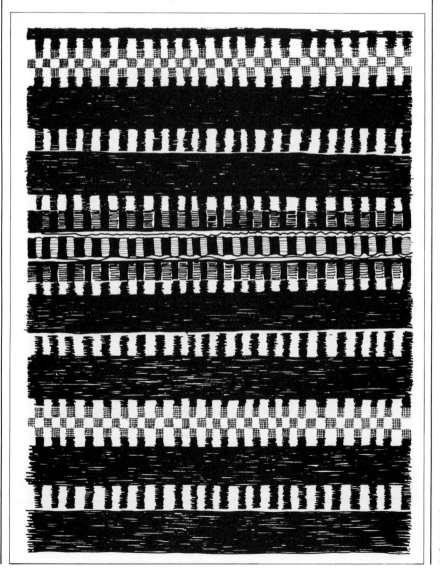

Inspirational illustration. A detail from a Czechoslovakian pillow case, woven in Eastern Slovakia in the late nineteenth century. The design is a 'Monk's Belt' weave.

Inspirational illustration. A pillow cover made in Czechoslovakia — the design is created by having coloured weft floats on a linen plain weave base.

closed, more specialised and more mechanised, until it eventually lost touch both physically and technically, with its cottage craft origins.

By the middle of the nineteenth century, what had once been a flexible growing intuitive craft had become a harsh industry. However that is not to say that the whole of European weaving was given over to industry, no, somehow or other, in a few isolated country areas the roots of the craft had survived and flourished. For example, in isolated nineteenth-century Wales and Scotland, in rural districts of such countries as Poland, Czechoslavakia and Scandinavia, pockets of folk weavers were still working much as they had always done.

The rest of the story is well documented — with the help of such craft revivalists as William Morris, Ruskin and later Ethel Mairet, we are now in the fortunate position of being able to relate to ancient weaving traditions and techniques. We are all part of this revival, with the very names and terms of the craft spanning time and linking us with our glorious past. For example, the word 'heddle' comes from an ancient Norse word meaning eye or chain, and the word 'lam' comes from an old Scandinavian word meaning to sweep or beat back. And then again, what could be more evocative than the very names of the weaves — Barley Corn, Monk's Belt, Rose Path, Goose Eye, Huck-a-Back and Honeysuckle. What more can we say except that if you work on this project, that is weaving a Monk's Belt design on a cottage loom and making a bedspread, you will be relating directly to the very roots of European weaving — it's an exciting and stimulating thought!

CONSIDERING THE PROJECT

If you have a look at the specifications for this project, plus of course the inspirational illustrations and the working drawings, you will see that we have chosen to work and weave on a largish, foot-powered, 4 shaft European type floor loom. Have a good close look at the drawings of the loom and note the relationship and placing of the jacks, heddles, lams, pedals, roller-beams and the top slung batten. The action of the loom is beautifully simple and direct, the pedals are pushed down with the foot, the cord linkage pulls down on the lams, the lams pull down on the jacks, and the jacks in turn, see-saw, and pull up the heddles. Now this loom may, in some way, be different from the loom that you now own, or the loom that you are thinking of buying, but no matter, the overall arrangement of your loom will, to a greater or lesser extent, be as described. Now having said this, it could be that your loom is some sort of 'special' type with extra pulleys, horses, counter-march harness and the like. Again not to worry, you will be able to adjust and modify our threading up to suit your loom.

We have chosen to work on a rising shed loom, because we feel the action is, broadly speaking, the same as on the table looms as used in previous projects; you push down, in this case with your foot, and the shed rises up — what could be easier or more straightforward? As to the project and the weave, certainly the Monk's Belt passage involves more pre-project planning and more complicated tying up and threading up, but that apart the warping is the same as already described in other projects. So to recap, the project is to weave and make a bedspread out of a 22 inch wide, 30 feet long length of cloth. This length has 25 feet of plain tabby weave, and 5 feet of Monk's Belt,

The working drawing grid — note the grid scale of seven grid squares to 1 inch. See how the 'Monk's Belt' weave is worded by having well organized blocks of weft floats.

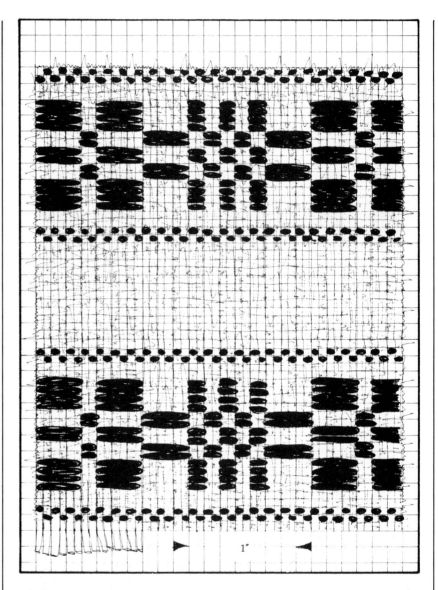

1"

weft-float patterning. See how the 30 feet of cloth is cut into three equal 10 feet lengths and arranged and sewn edge to edge to make up the bedspread.

Now cast your eyes over the specifications and note the possible order of weaving alternatives. For example, on the 32 feet warp you could first weave say $2\frac{1}{2}$ feet of tabby, then the 5 feet of Monk's Belt, and then finally another $22\frac{1}{2}$ feet of tabby. However, we have chosen to weave the $22\frac{1}{2}$ feet of tabby first, and then to follow this up with the 5 feet decorative panel and the final $2\frac{1}{2}$ feet of tabby. Our thinking behind this way of working is simple, we reckon that by the time you have woven the $22\frac{1}{2}$ feet of tabby, you will understand and appreciate all the little quirks of your loom and so be better able to cope with the more complicated Monk's Belt passage.

As to the yarn, we've gone for a medium fine, warp-strength wool and use this for both the warp and weft — for the patterned areas we use the same weight and type of yarn, just a different colour. The warp is sett at 14 ends to the inch with string heddles and a 7 dent reed. Now if you look closely at the working drawings you will see that there are twenty-five 1½ inch Monk's Belt bands of pattern in all, and that they are interspaced with 1 inch bands of plain tabby to make a total pattern area of about 61½ inches.

MATERIALS

For weaving this 22 inch wide, 30 feet long piece of tabby cloth with weft-float decoration, and allowing for all the usual loom extras, we have calculated that you'll need at least 24,000 feet of yarn, medium fine wool, as described. For the decorative weft, you will need about 1000 feet of yarn — we've chosen dark blue so as to contrast the plain cream of the tabby weave.

TOOLS AND EQUIPMENT

For this project you will need the use of a largish floor loom; we've chosen to use a foot-powered European/American loom, one with back and front roller-beams, a rising shed action, string heddles, 4 shafts and 6 pedals. Note you will only be using four pedals, so you might use a four pedal loom. As

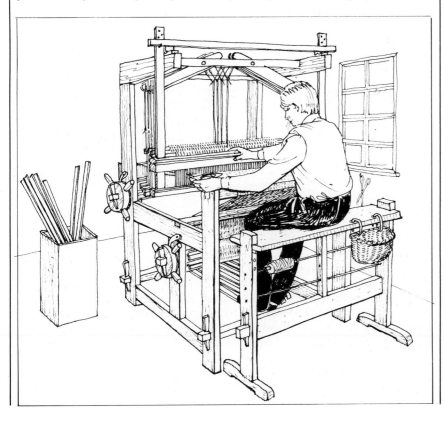

The loom — note how our loom has a spool rack under the bench seat, and a seat basket close at hand for bobbins, shuttles, a tape measure, scissors and such like. See also how the batten is firmly grasped and swung, and how with a long warp, sticks are placed at the front roller between layers of woven cloth.

for all the back-up equipment, you will need a raddle to suit the loom, a 7 dent reed, a collection of shed sticks, at least two roller boat type shuttles, a reed hook, a warping frame, a bobbin winder, and of course you will need all the usual bits and pieces like scissors, pencils, workout paper, a calculator, etc.

PREPARING THE WARP

If you look at the details and illustrations, you will see that we are working this warp on a pegged frame — this isn't the ideal piece of equipment for such a long warp, you might better use individual pegs and clamps, or a large

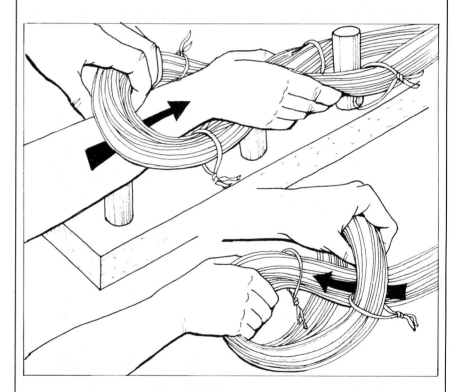

When you have built the half-warps on the frame, loop them into a chain for easy handling.

warping mill (see Data section). However start by setting out the warping frame with a 32 feet cotton warp guide, arrange the cord so that there's a three-peg cross at each end of the warp. Note that at 14 ends to the inch, and extra selvedge threads, there are a total of 312 warps. Bearing this in mind, run your warp yarn backwards and forwards through the frame until you have made two well-established and tied half-warps-each with 156 threads. Note — because this warp is long, it's all the more important that it be well tied; we suggest that you have a generous number of cross-ties at each end of the warp, and ties at about every foot or so along its length. Now very carefully slip one end of the warp off the cross-pegs, pass your hand through the loop, then make a tidy warp-chain, as illustrated

PUTTING THE WARP ON THE LOOM

First clear away the warping frame, then set out all your tools. Now take a shed stick and a cord, and secure one end of the warp to the back roller-beam as shown in most of the other projects. This done, set the card covered raddle across the back of the loom, then grasp and temporarily tie all the string heddles so that they are collected at the centre of the loom. Now take the two half-warps, one each side of the bunched heddle strings, and pass them forward to the front of the loom. Next remove the ties from the back end of the warp, and carefully spread the threads in the raddle so that they are set to the full 22 inch width. When you are sure that all is correct, clip the top on the raddle and secure it with a couple of cords.

Now get your helper to stand at the front of the loom, and to unchain as

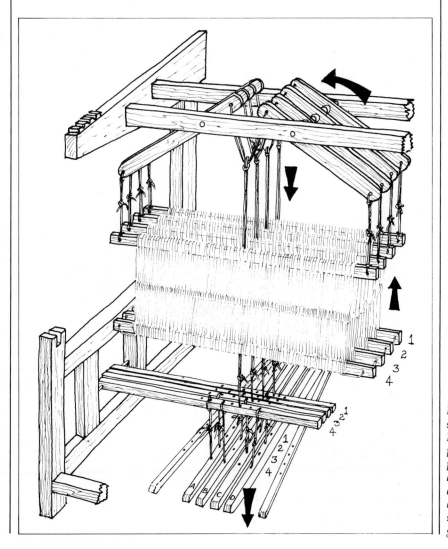

Diagram showing the mechanism of a rising shed jack loom and the tying order. Note: Pedal 'A' is tied to lams/harness 4 and 3, pedal 'B' is tied to lams/harness 4 and 2, pedal 'C' is tied to lams and harness 3 and 1, and pedal 'D' is tied to lams and harness 2 and 4. See how when the pedals are pressed down, the lams come down, the seesaw jacks swing down and the heddle shafts/harnesses go up.

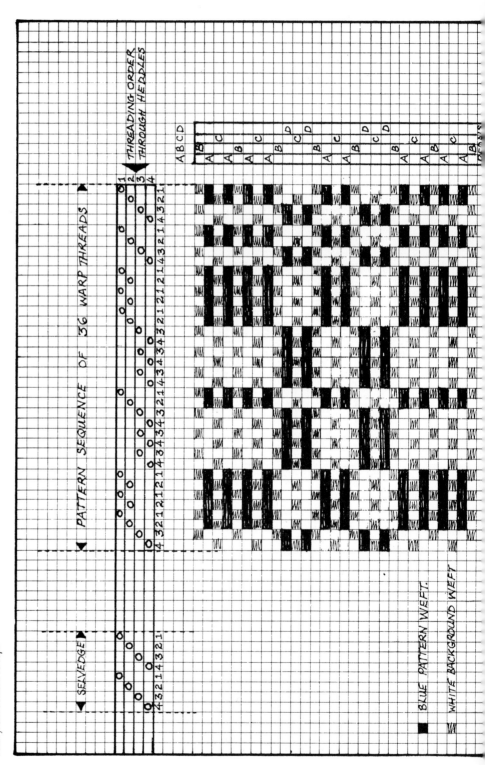

The threading and drafting plan for the 'Monk's Belt' weave. The pedalling order is read from bottom to top.

much warp as space allows. This done, your helper can now take the strain, and pull on the warp, while you, at one and the same time, wind the warp onto the back roller. As the warp is being wound on, place shed sticks between the roller-beam and the warp layers, and also keep an eye on the warp as it is being combed through the raddle — watch out that threads don't tangle, knot or break. Note — this warp is tricky only because it is long — work with co-ordinated care and caution, and try all the while to wind-on and tension with a constant even action. Continue to wind-on and remove warp ties until the front end of the warp is about level with the front roller-beam.

Now push two shed sticks through the front warp cross, as illustrated in other projects, then remove the final cross-ties, ease the cross towards the back of the loom, and then remove the raddle. Now cut the front warp loops, and tie them in place to the front of the loom with a couple of lark's head knots. Finally, place 'praying' hands through the centre of the bunch of heddles, and sweep them left and right so that they are hard up against the secured warp and the sides of the loom.

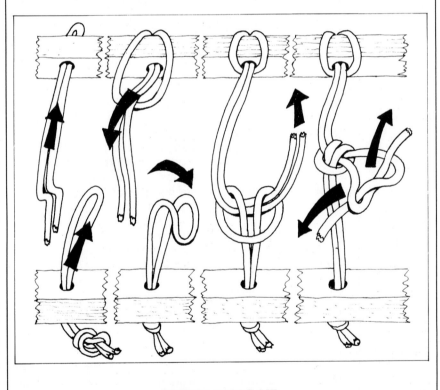

The knot used for attaching the heddles to the pedals and jacks — the sequence is read from left to right.

THREADING UP

Have a long slow look at the various working drawings and detailed illustrations, and see how the pattern runs and how the loom is organised. Now to work — take note, you will be using 4 shafts, meaning all four sets of heddles, but you will only be using four of the six pedals — it might help if

When you come to threading up the string heddles, it's a good idea to actually number your fingers 1, 2, 3, 4, you can then grasp the half-warp that is to be threaded, and at the same time push numbered fingers through the heddles — it all makes for easy handling.

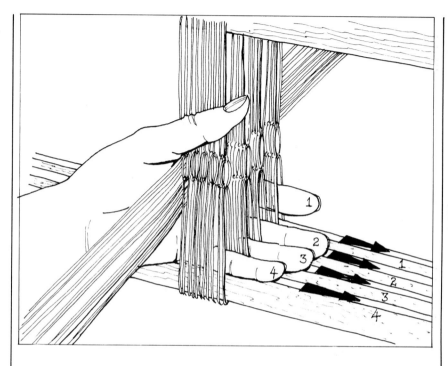

you tie the two outside pedals out of the way, Now this next step is critical, so be warned — with masking tape and a marker, label the pedals from left to right so that they read, 'A', 'B', 'C' and 'D', and now label the heddle shafts and lams from the back of the loom to the front, so that they are numbered, '1', '2', '3' and '4'. Before you go any further look at the Monk's Belt threading or draft plan, as illustrated, and see how the total pattern width is made up of eight 36-thread repeats, and two selvedge areas each with twelve threads.

Starting with the left-hand half-warp, focus your attention on the threads as they occur at the cross. Now working from the centre of the loom, thread the heddles up in the following four-thread sequence, 1, 2, 3, 4,/1, 2, 3, 4,/1, 2, 1, 2,/1, 2, 3, 4,/3, 4, 3, 4,/1, 2, 3, 4,/3, 4, 3, 4,/1, 2, 1, 2,/1, 2, 3, 4. When you come to the end of this first 36-thread sequence, and you have checked and tied every little block of four threads, then repeat the 36-thread sequence three more times in like manner.

Eventually, when you have worked four sequences, you will be left with twelve threads, thread the first four in the order 1, 2, 3 and 4, then double up the last eight, and run these also in the order 1, 2, 3 and 4. When you have threaded up the left-hand half-warp, then work the right-hand half-warp in the same way, that is threading up four 36-thread sequences and the twelve thread selvedge, but this time run the sequences from the centre of the loom in the reverse order 4, 3, 2, 1,/2, 1, 2, 1,/4, 3, 4, 3,/4, 3, 2, 1,/4, 3, 4, 3,/4, 3, 2, 1,/2, 1, 2, 1,/4, 3, 2, 1,/4, 3, 2, 1. This sequence should be repeated four times, then finally run the last selvedge threads in the order, 4, 3, 2, 1 and 4, 3, 2, 1, as already described.

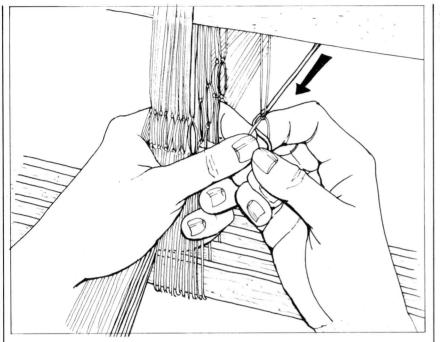

Heddles are threaded up in order, with the numbered fingers working their own batch of numbered heddles.

When you have checked and re-checked the threading order and you are happy that all is correct, put the 7 dent reed in its frame, find its centre, then working from the centre of the reed outwards to the sides of the loom, pass the ordered warp threads, in pairs, through the reed dents/slots. Note — at the selvedge, run the last eight warps at four to a slot.

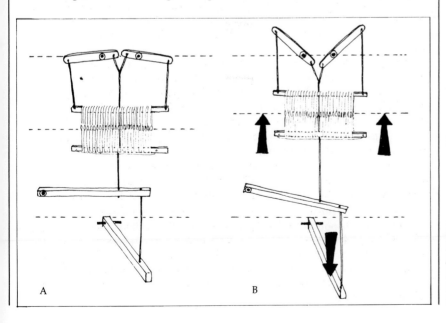

A   B

The loom linkage/action. (A) the pedal and harness at the 'rest' position. (B) the pedal and harness at the 'working' position — see how the pedal pulls down the lam, which in turn pulls down one end of the jack, which in turn pulls the harness/warp threads up.

Tying up the pedals for the 'Monk's Belt' weave, pedal A goes to heddles/lams 4 and 3, pedal B goes to heddles/lams 4 and 2, pedal C to 3 and 1, and pedal D to 2 and 4.

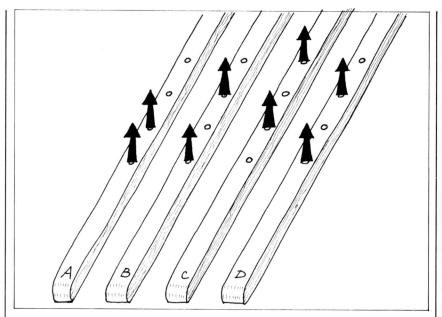

Again, as you work, pass and check each small group of threads through the reed slots and tie and secure the groups with slip knots.

Finally, tie a warp/shed stick to the front roller-beam, stroke the total warp towards the front of the loom, and tie-up and tension, as described in the other projects.

TYING UP THE PEDALS

Have a look at our working drawings, and see how with our loom there is a direct cord linkage between the four heddle shafts and the four lams. So now working the pedals from left to right in the order A, B, C, D tie the lam cords to the pedals. The tie-up order of pedals to lams is as follows, pedal 'A' is tied to lams 4 and 3, pedal 'B' tied to 4 and 2, pedal 'C' is tied to 3 and 1, and finally pedal 'D' is tied to lams 2 and 4. This done, adjust the warp tension and the various pedal, lam and heddle cords, until the loom action is smooth and positive, and the sheds are clear and well set up. Note — adjust the tying-up until, with all sheds, the 'down' threads gently rest on the 'beating-back beam', the batten, (see Data section).

WEAVING

First check the threading order and the loom adjustment by running a coloured yarn through the various tabby and Monk's Belt sheds. For a plain tabby weave, press the pedals 'B' and 'C' alternately, and for the Monk's Belt use pedals 'A' and 'D' alternately, or according to the pattern. When you are certain that all's well, take your weft yarn, all nicely contained in the roller shuttle, (see previous project), and using pedals 'B' and 'C' alternately, weave away. The plain tabby is simple and uncomplicated, the action is,

The weaving action is, press down on the pedal so that the shed opens, and the lower warp threads rest on the shuttle race, then throw the shuttle through the shed so that the weft sits freely, then beat back with the batten.

press down 'B' so that heddles 4 and 2 rise, pass through the weft, close down and beat back. Now press down pedal 'C' so that heddles 3 and 1 rise, pass through the weft, close down and beat back. And so you continue working pedals 'B' and 'C' alternately.

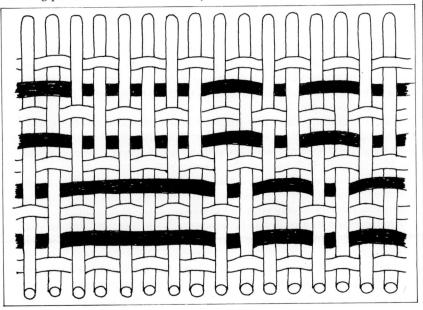

A detail of the decorative and base weave — see how the tabby weave is constant throughout, and note how the decorative threads skip/float over the warp.

When you get to the patterned area, things get a little more difficult because not only are you running alternate tabby pedals, but you are also running the pattern pedals. Now bearing in mind that tabby is worked by pedals 'B' and 'C', and the Monk's Belt by 'A' and 'D' for the design as illustrated, run the pedals in the order, <u>B</u>, A, <u>C</u>, A, <u>B</u>, A, <u>C</u>, A, <u>B</u>, D, <u>C</u>, D, <u>B</u>, A, <u>C</u>, A, <u>B</u>, D, <u>C</u>, D, <u>B</u>, A, <u>C</u>, A, <u>B</u>, A, <u>C</u>, A, <u>B</u>. Note how the tabby weave (the letters underlined) remain constant throughout the pattern weave.

When you come to weaving the bands of pattern, we must emphasise that the tabby is being worked, as it were, behind the Monk's Belt floats, as well as between the bands of pattern. See how there are twenty-five bands of pattern, each interspaced with a 1 inch band of tabby.

Of course with a project of this type and complexity, you are almost certainly going to make a few mistakes, but as long as you remember that when you come to the patterned areas, to run both the tabby weave and the Monk's Belt alternately, then your mistakes are only going to be small ones.

FINISHING AND MAKING UP

When you have woven the full 30 feet or so of warp, cut the cloth from the loom and free it from all sticks and strings. Now take a needle and darn in all the loose weft and warp ends. This done, have a look at the working drawings and see how the bedspread is made up of three 10 feet lengths, and see also how the 5 feet piece of pattern occurs at the centre of the bedspread.

Now place, pin and tack the three lengths of cloth so that they are as illustrated, and then using the weft yarn and an over-and-over stitch, sew them edge to edge. Finally, hem the top and bottom of the bedspread, and then soak, scour, mill and press, as described in the Data section.

AFTERTHOUGHTS AND TIPS

We have worked this project on a rising shed loom, meaning when the pedals go down, the heddle shafts go up. Your loom might have balanced shafts, counter-marches or whatever; if you are a raw beginner it might be a good idea to experiment and get to grips with the complexities of this project on a small table loom.

We have used a medium fine woollen yarn, a yarn of warp-strength — you might use cotton, linen or whatever, but still stay with the same warp and weft weight and spacing. Note, the weft wrapped round a ruler covers about 18–20 ends to the inch run (see Data section).

When you are weaving, aim for an easy natural rhythm; when you have got into the swing of things, measure an inch of weft, and count the lines of weft yarn, then try to stay with this density.

After every foot of cloth has been woven, lay in a tag of coloured wool at the selvedge, then at a glance you will know how much cloth you have woven.

When you come to adjust the various loom ties and cords prior to weaving, you will need a helper sitting at the loom. Ask your helper to press down on the pedals in turn, and to run through the various shed combinations; adjust

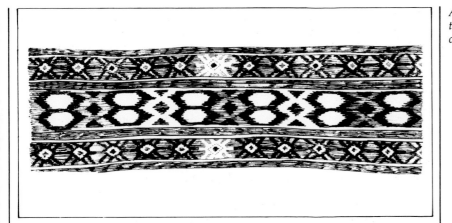

A detail from an Albanian brocaded towel — the design is worked in grey, white and red cotton.

lam, heddle and pedal cords, so that with all the sheds the 'down' warps rest, without undue strain on the batten/beater.

BIBLIOGRAPHY

ON WEAVING
Albers, Anni   Published by Studio Vista, 1966

NAVAJO WEAVING
Amsden, Avery C.   Published by Peregrine Smith Inc, 1975

BYWAYS IN HANDWEAVING
Atwater, M. M.   Published by Macmillan, New York, 1968

THE TECHNIQUE OF WOVEN TAPESTRY
Beutlick, Tadek   Published by Batsford, 1967

KEY TO WEAVING
Black, Mary E.   Published by Bruce, Milwaukee, 1945

VILLAGE ARTS OF ROMANIA
British Museum   Published by British Museum, 1971

KEEP ME WARM ONE NIGHT; EARLY HANDWEAVING IN E. CANADA
Burnham, Harold B. and Dorothy K.   Published by University of Toronto Press, 1973

TEXTILES OF ANCIENT PERU AND THEIR TECHNIQUES
D'Harcourt, Raoul   Published by University of Washington Press

SAMISK BANDVEVNAD FRA FINNMARK
Haugen, Anny   Published by Forlagt, 1946

INDIAN BLANKETS AND THEIR MAKERS
James, Wharton G.   Published by Dover, USA, 1974

INTRODUCING WEST AFRICAN CLOTH
Kent, Kate P.   Published by Denver Museum, 1971

DESIGNING ON THE LOOM
Kirby, Mary   Published by Studio, 1955

WEST AFRICAN WEAVING
Lamb, Venice   Published by Duckworth, 1976

RUG WEAVING
Lewes, Klares and Hutton, Helen   Published by Batsford, 1962

HANDWEAVING TODAY
Mairet, Ethel   Published by Faber and Faber, London, 1939

NAVAJO TECHNIQUES FOR TODAY'S WEAVERS
Mattera, Joan   Published by Watson and Guptill/Pitman, 1975/1976

TEXTILES OF HIGHLAND GUATEMALA
O'Neale, Lil M.   Published by Carnegie Institution, Washington, 1945

PEASANT ART IN ROUMANIA
Oprescu, George   Published by Studio, London, 1929

WEAVING A NAVAJO BLANKET
Reichard, Glays A.   Published by Dover, 1974

CRAFTS OF MEXICO
Sayer, Chloe   Published by Aldus Books, London, 1977

AFRICAN TEXTILES AND DECORATIVE ARTS
Sieber, Roy   Published by Museum of Modern Art, New York, 1972

THE WEAVERS CRAFT
Simpson, L. E. and Weir, M.   Published by Dryad, 1946

THE McDOUGALL COLLECTION OF INDIAN TEXTILES FROM GUATEMALA AND MEXICO
Start, Laura E.   Published by Oxford University Press, 1948

THE FOLK ARTS OF NORWAY
Stewart, Janice S.   Published by Dover, 1972

THE CRAFT OF THE WEAVER
Sutton, Anne, Collingwood, Peter and St Aubyn, Hubbard   Published by BBC, 1982

BACKSTRAP WEAVING
Taber, B and Anderson, M.   Published by Pitman, 1975

THE TECHNIQUE OF WEAVING
Tovey, John   Published by Batsford, 1965

AFRICAN DESIGN
Trowell, M.   Published in London, 1966.

INDEX

How to make the most of your talents...

...get POPULAR CRAFTS every month

United Kingdom	**£17.90**
Overseas (Surface Mail)	**£21.50**
	or U.S. **$28.00**
Overseas (Air Mail)	**£40.00**

If you would like to subscribe to POPULAR CRAFTS, please make your cheque, postal order or international money order payable to ARGUS SPECIALIST PUBLICATIONS LTD, or send your Access/Barclaycard number to the following address or telephone your credit card order on 0442 48432.

Send your remittance to:
INFONET LTD., Times House, 179 The Marlowes, Hemel Hempstead, Herts. HP1 1BB.